Advance Praise for
Preaching from Hebrews

MW00835122

Several years ago, after James Earl Massey spoke at our seminary, one of my students followed me out of the chapel service to ask, "How can I become that kind of preacher?" I couldn't give a succinct answer but this book is a good step in that direction. *Preaching from Hebrews* demonstrates Dr. Massey's love for the Scriptures, his meticulous scholarship, and his creative homiletical insights. Any careful reader will come out a better preacher.

> J. Ellsworth Kalas
> Senior Professor of Homiletics
> Asbury Theological Seminary

Preaching from Hebrews is a masterpiece of seasoned insights from the esteemed biblical scholar and master preacher James Earl Massey… Massey takes us inside the mind of the author of Hebrews and showcases the preaching prowess and interpretive genius of this first-century follow of Jesus. No one who can offer a more comprehensive and compelling look at Hebrews than James Earl Massey. This is a "must read" for all students of the Bible and all preachers. It will make you want to preach from Hebrews!

> Curtiss Paul DeYoung
> Professor of Reconciliation Studies
> Bethel University

As an exegetical surgeon, Dr. James Earl Massey carefully and precisely dissects the book of Hebrews and produces a commentary that is both biblically and theologically preachable. In *Preaching from Hebrews*, Massey demonstrates an intimate understanding and ready use of scripture in centering the book of Hebrews within the overall plan and comprehensive purpose of the whole counsel of God. His functional and applicable employment of the Greek language along with his special occasion sermons from various texts within the book of Hebrews make this volume a necessity and not merely a luxury for those who are serious about rightly dividing the Word of truth.

Robert Smith, Jr.

Professor of Christian Preaching

Beeson Divinity School

In *Preaching from Hebrews*, James Earl Massey brings together his unique skills as a biblical scholar and homiletician to create a new and different kind of book. In Part One, Massey provides an insightful commentary into the Book of Hebrews. In Part Two, he looks at Hebrews through the eyes of a preacher, bringing to bear his considerable skills as a one of the most significant homileticians of his age. This book enables today's preachers to do quality exegesis in Hebrews and provides understanding about how context matters, how preaching themes can be developed, and how sermons can be produced from those ideas and themes. Massey provides examples from some of the greatest preachers who have ever lived and practical examples from his own preaching work. In the end, Massey's greatest gift in this book may be to foster a new template for how preaching books should be written. I recommend it to all who want to grow in their preaching skills.

Jeffery W. Frymire
Associate Professor of Homiletics
Asbury Theological Seminary
(Orlando)

My friend James Earl Massey loves the book of Hebrews. Get into this notebook of research findings and see for yourself! His years of in-depth study, with the intent of preaching from Hebrews, have yielded bountiful fruit in this volume. He takes pains to unearth theological and historical detail, then uses his discoveries to create a valuable resource for announcing the Good News.

Donald A. Demaray
Emeritus Professor of Preaching
Asbury Theological Seminary

Dr. Massey has given us a short guide to preaching from Hebrews that takes the history of the book and its place in the New Testament canon seriously. By carefully chosen examples, he shows us what can be done to make the text live in the lives of God's people today. A great achievement.

Gerald T. Bray
Research Professor
Beeson Divinity School

This extraordinary study of the Letter to the Hebrews is an exhilarating pilgrimage into the heart and mind of James Earl Massey. His seasoned embodiment of the vocation of biblical hermeneutics and homiletics bears fresh witness to the challenge of preaching Christ to diverse audiences in modern times.

Cheryl J. Sanders
Professor Christian Ethics
Howard University School of Divinity

PREACHING
from
HEBREWS
HERMENEUTICAL INSIGHTS & HOMILETICAL HELPS

JAMES EARL MASSEY

Warner Press

CONNECT • EQUIP • INSPIRE

ANDERSON, INDIANA

For this and all other editorial matters, please contact the Editorial Director. To purchase additional copies of this book, to inquire about distribution, and for all other sales-related matters, please contact the Sales Department.

Warner Press, Inc.
PO Box 2499
Anderson, IN 46018-2499
800-741-7721
www.warnerpress.org

ISBN-13: 978-1-59317-664-8 (pbk)
ISBN-13: 978-1-59317-665-5 (EPUB)
ISBN-13: 978-1-59317-666-2 (Kindle)

Printed in the United States of America.

14 15 16 17 18 19 20 /VP/ 10 9 8 7 6 5 4 3 2 1

Dedicated to the memory of

Thomas Samuel Kepler (1897–1963)

Charles H. Shaw (1898–1987)

Herbert Gordon May (1904–1977)

and Raymond S. Brown, S.S. (1928–1998)

esteemed biblical scholars

my teachers

who honored and aided my quest

to understand and use

both Testaments in vital relation.

Contents

Foreword

James Earl Massey holds together two traits that ought to characterize every minister of the Gospel but that often seem lacking or disjointed today: gravity and grace. Although he has a great sense of humor, there is nothing frivolous or cheaply funny about him. His words carry weight. He is a person of serious intent, and his preaching is marked by purpose. In a culture where words are frequently inflated, defaced, and manipulated, in a world where "words strain, crack, and sometimes break," as T. S. Eliot put it, Massey speaks with clarity and eloquence—and out of the depths.

Such *gravitas*, in pulpit, pen, and personal devotion is balanced with a grace-filled life of service to Jesus Christ and his church. This is evident to all who know James Earl Massey, and I have known him well as friend and mentor for more than twenty-five years. His long and varied ministry has been marked by what St. Paul called "the fruit of the Spirit" (Gal 5:22). His spirituality—deep but not pretentious—shines through in his demeanor and discipline, in his humility, compassion, and consideration of others. True godliness is the byproduct of having lived and walked with Jesus. It is evident that this is the source of both Massey's character and his calling.

Massey is a master communicator in pulpit and classroom alike. He has served both church and academy in diverse roles and settings. For twenty-two years he served as senior pastor of the Metropolitan Church of God in Detroit, a congregation he founded in 1954, the year of *Brown v. Board of Education*. His commitment to human dignity for every person made in the image of God and to civil rights for every citizen of the land was shaped by Martin Luther King Jr., his colleague and friend, and by Howard Thurman, his mentor and inspiration.

Massey's voice became known throughout the world—and this is how he first influenced me—as the speaker on the "Christian Brotherhood Hour," the international radio broadcast of his denomination, the Church of God (Anderson). His work as a missionary educator in Jamaica shaped his perspective on life outside of the country where he was born. His labors as dean of the chapel of Tuskegee University (1984–1989) and dean of Anderson School of Theology (1989–1995) have left an enduring legacy for good at both institutions.

The listing of these assignments reveals much about the pilgrimage of James Earl Massey, but not everything. While deeply anchored in the Wesleyan theology and the Holiness traditions of his own denomination, Massey's ministry has reached across the universal Body of Christ. In 1966, he participated in the World Congress on Evangelism held in Berlin and co-chaired by Billy Graham and Carl F. H. Henry. This conference was a forerunner of the Lausanne Movement for World Evangelization, which was launched in 1974 with Massey again taking a leading role.

Over the years, Massey has served the church well as a scholar and writer of distinction. His more than twenty books have covered a wide range of pastoral theology (especially homiletics), biblical scholarship, and spiritual uplift. He has also written for numerous magazines and periodicals and has served as a senior editor at *Christianity Today*. His work continues strong today with new publications and numerous invitations to preach and present lectures in churches and schools, large and small, across the breadth of this country and beyond.

And now we have from the pen of James Earl Massey another book of theological depth and biblical wisdom, *Preaching from Hebrews: Hermeneutical Insights and Homiletical Helps*. In some ways, this study is the culmination of a lifelong interest in the Epistle to the Hebrews. Of all the books in the New Testament, Hebrews is the one that best illuminates the Old Testament in light of the New. At the same time, it is also the one most shrouded in mystery, for there is much about it that we do not know: Who wrote it?

When was it written? For which community of believers was it intended? Why was there so much debate about its canonicity in the early church?

Massey reviews these historical and critical issues, but his primary focus is on the epistle's central theme: the supremacy of Jesus Christ. In Hebrews, temptation is real, sin is serious, atonement is necessary, salvation is abundant, and all of this flows from one of the highest Christologies in all of early Christian literature. In Hebrews, Jesus brings a superior covenant, a better sanctuary, and a new life of discipleship shaped by faith and holiness.

Massey delves deeply into the rich theology of this important letter, but his real aim is to offer practical help to the preaching pastor by showing how one moves from text to sermon. In his *Homiletics*, Karl Barth wrote that authentic preaching should not only be *about* the Bible but also *from* the Bible. Massey demonstrates here exactly how that works.

In this closely textured study of the epistle to the Hebrews, Massey has brought together several genres of writing: literary analysis, historical overview, theological exposition, biblical commentary, and a manual for preaching. The many books James Earl Massey has written across the years fill one of the most often-turned-to shelves in my own library, and I am eager to add this one to it. *Preaching from Hebrews*, I predict, will become an enduring masterpiece.

Several years ago I offered the following tribute to Dr. Massey. The words still ring right today:

> While many people seek greatness but only attain mediocrity, James Earl Massey has been lifted to greatness while seeking simply to be faithful to his calling. Beyond his many accomplishments, at the core of Dr. Massey's being there is an essential decency, humility, and spirituality that is compelling. Never one to give himself to minor abso-

lutes, he has modeled, with courage and compassion, the burdensome joy of a herald whose life reflects the message he proclaims. In the words of the great Howard Thurman, his life is "a great rejoicing!"

Timothy George

Timothy George is founding dean of Beeson Divinity School of Samford University and general editor of the *Reformation Commentary of Scripture.*

Preface

The Letter to the Hebrews is one of the most intriguing books within the New Testament and an important bridge book between the two Testaments. In a way that is unparalleled by any other New Testament writing, this letter captures strategic accents of the Christian gospel and applies them with aptness to highlight how the exalted Christ ministers to believers struggling with the demanding details of life. When this message is rightly understood and aptly treated in teaching and preaching, there can result a deepened appreciation for the ongoing ministry of Jesus, a quickened faith in God, and a settled commitment for faithful living as a Christian pilgrim.

This book is for those who seek help toward understanding the letter to the Hebrews and who desire to use it in teaching and preaching. Thus, there is extended treatment of historical matters and the central theological perspectives found in the letter before guidance is offered about how to preach from it. Commentary on the message of the Letter is given as Unit Reflections in Chapter 2; the intent has been to sharpen the focus of the text and expose the theological flavor and force its *Auctor* supplied. The sermons supplied in this book are all based on the New Revised Standard Version (1989) or its immediate predecessor, the Revised Standard Version.

This book is an expanded treatment of the Newell Lectures in Biblical Studies given in 1986 at Anderson School of Theology. The lectures were afterward expanded for a course on Hebrews that I taught as a Visiting Professor of Preaching at Princeton Theological Seminary in 1987. Some of these materials were used again in 1992 during the Annual Conference on Preaching at Southern Baptist Theological Seminary; in 1994 at Princeton University during sessions there of the American Academy of

Ministry; during the 13th Annual Samford University Pastor's School at Beeson Divinity School in July 2000; and in a January 2003 course on Hebrews at Beeson Divinity School. The welcome given the presentations by so many working pastors and graduate students confirmed anew in me the importance of sharing these hermeneutical and homiletical helps on a wider scale. Thus this book.

It only remains for me to report that the unit reflections that appear as chapter 2 were first published in an earlier form as serial pieces in *Vital Christianity* magazine (May–July issues, 1986) under the heading "Jesus and the Believer: Studies in the Letter to the Hebrews." They were later published as the commentary section on Hebrews in *True to Our Native Land: An African American New Testament Commentary* (ed. Brian K. Blount et al. [Minneapolis: Fortress Press, 2007], pp 444–60). I am grateful both to Warner Press, Inc., and to Fortress Press for granting permission to re-use the reflections in expanded form as part of this book.

James Earl Massey

Part I: Hebrews in Focus

Chapter 1:

The History and Influence of Hebrews in Early Church Life

I. Hebrews in Early Church Life

Who the first recipients of the Letter to Hebrews were cannot be answered with unquestioned certainty, but the presence of so many sentences and phrases from it in First Clement, another church document usually dated around AD 96, argues well that believers living in Rome might have been the letter's original target audience. Written by one Clement of Rome, a major leader in the church there ca. AD 90–100, First Clement is a letter sent by the church at Rome to the church at Corinth after learning about some troubles there that needed correcting. The salutation begins, "The Church of God which sojourns in Rome to the Church of God which sojourns in Corinth," but the writing person, tradition maintains, was one Clement, who was either the pastor or the leading elder in the church at Rome.[1]

Clement was profoundly influenced by the thoughts and expressions in the Letter to Hebrews, and his letter to Corinth uses actual quotations from the writing and makes distinct allusions to its message, all of which

---

1. Irenaeus of Lyon (ca. 175–ca. 202) referred to Clement as Bishop in Rome "in the third place from the apostles" (perhaps meaning that after the apostolic leadership supplied there by Peter and Paul, Clement followed Linus and Anacletus). See his *Against Heresies*, III.iii.3.

evidences that the Letter to Hebrews was one of his resources.[2] The following list of references provides a ready set of these correspondences.

First Clement	Hebrews
7:1	12:1–2
9:3	11:5
9:4	11:7
17:1	11:37
17:5	3:5
19:2	12:1
21:9	4:12
27:1	10:23
27:2	6:18
27:4	11:3
36:1	2:17,18; 4:14,15; 8:3
36:2	1:3,4; 6:4f
36:3	1:7 (Ps 103:4)
36:4	1:5 (Ps 2:7–8)
36:5	1:13 (Ps 110:1)
48:8	12:23
63:1	12:1f

2. For an extended study of all the scriptures Clement used in his writing, see Donald A. Hagner, *The Use of the Old and New Testament in Clement of Rome* (Leiden, Netherlands: E. J. Brill, 1973); see especially pp. 179–95 for Clement's use of the Hebrews letter. See also Edgar J. Goodspeed, *New Solutions of New Testament Problems* (Chicago: University of Chicago Press, 1927), pp. 110–15; Ceslas Spicq, *L'Epitre aux Hebreux*, Vol 1 (Paris: J. Gabalda, 1952), pp. 177–78.

The traditional dating of ca. AD 96 places First Clement within the sub-Apostolic period, a time within the last one-third of the first century, just thirty or so years after the death of Peter and Paul. If the tradition that Tertullian (ca. 155–220) reported is accepted, namely that Peter was the one who ordained Clement,[3] then the document Clement wrote is the work of an immediate follower of that apostle. In First Clement 5:1b, Peter and Paul are lauded as "noble examples of our own generation," indicating closeness to them in time and, some believe, that Clement was acquainted with the two apostles. That both Peter and Paul were now dead is clear from Clement's words about each: "[Peter] having thus given his testimony went to the glorious place which was his due" (5:4); "[Paul] taught righteousness to all the world, and when he had reached the limits of the West he gave his testimony before the rulers, and thus passed from the world and was taken up into the Holy Place—the greatest example of endurance" (5:7).[4]

If Tertullian was correct in reporting that Peter ordained Clement, and since First Clement borrowed so readily from Hebrews, then it might well be presumed that the Letter to Hebrews was written by someone who had also known Peter and/or Paul, as Clement did. While this possibility should not be stated dogmatically as fact, one thing is clear: the borrowing Clement did from Hebrews as he wrote does suggest that the Hebrews letter was known within the setting of the church at Rome before the end of the first century.

A second important source in tracing the history and influence of the Letter to Hebrews in the early church is the ancient ten-volume *Ecclesiastical History* of Eusebius Pamphili (ca. 260–ca. 339), bishop

---

3. Tertullian, *Prescription of Heretics* 32:1–2.
4. Quotations from First Clement are from *The Apostolic Fathers*, Vol. 1, trans. by Kirsopp Lake (Cambridge, MA: Harvard University Press, 1912), Loeb Classical Library edition.

of Caesarea. Writing to give a detailed report of the succession of orthodox leaders and teachings of the church at a time when heretical and deviant groups were multiplying and bringing the Christian faith under increased attack by critics, Eusebius traced the course of orthodoxy in the most prominent regions of the Empire world and identified as well those persons and groups responsible for erroneous and divisive teachings.

Published in its final form in AD 325, the *Ecclesiastical History* treats in chronological order the major leaders, events, fortunes, and problems at four major centers of the church from the time of its founding after the resurrection of Jesus down to the time of Eusebius, its writer. Book 1 tells about the earthly ministry of Jesus Christ; Book 2 reports the activities of the apostles and tells how Peter and Paul died. In Book 3, Eusebius reports the traditions about which writings were used in the churches as a basis for teaching, worship, and personal edification, and which writings were either questioned or rejected. In reporting those traditions, Eusebius referred repeatedly to those who were his predecessors in ministry, and many statements from them about the Letter to Hebrews appear in the history he prepared.

The student of *Ecclesiastical History* will notice Eusebius's very useful method of treating the same topic or event more than once and the strategy he demonstrated in repeating certain comments and aspects of history in order to shed light on the different periods he covered in reporting about the ongoing history of the church. With respect to authoritative writings, Eusebius stated this as his planned method of reporting about them:

> I will take pains to indicate successively which of the orthodox writers in each period used any of the doubtful books, and what they said about the canonical [*endiathekon*]

and accepted [*homologoumenon*] Scriptures and what about those which are not such.[5]

In applying this method to what his predecessors had to report about the Letter to the Hebrews, Eusebius began with a presumably early accounting of how the church at Rome viewed the work: "And the fourteen letters of Paul are obvious and plain, yet it is not right to ignore that some dispute the Epistle to the Hebrews, saying that it was rejected by the church of Rome as not being by Paul, and I will expound at the proper time what was said about it by our predecessors."[6]

By "our predecessors," Eusebius meant certain major leaders honored in the Eastern church: Clement of Alexandria (ca. 155–ca. 220); Origen (ca. 185–ca. 254); and Dionysius the Great (died. ca. 264), bishop of Alexandria from 247 to 264.[7] Although Eusebius reported traditions from Western church leaders, it seems that he favored Eastern church views—probably influenced by his schooling under the leaders there—and his comments on the opinions of the leaders there are usually more extensive.

In Book 3 of his *Ecclesiastical History,* Eusebius reported on the recognition accorded the Epistle of Clement (=First Clement) and mentioned as commonly known fact that its writer had borrowed heavily from the Letter to the Hebrews:

---

5. Eusebius, *Ecclesiastical History*, Bk. III:iii.3. One of the better study editions is supplied by Loeb Classical Library: Vol. 1, English translation by Kirsopp Lake (Cambridge, MA: Harvard University Press, 1926); Vol. 2, English translation by H. J. Lawlor and John E. L. Oulton (Cambridge, MA: Harvard University Press, 1932).

6. *Ecclesiastical History*, Bk. III.iii.5.

7. In Bk. VII.l, Eusebius referred to Dionysius as "the great bishop of the Alexandrians," a clear indication of his esteem for that church leader whom he quoted so often and approvingly. Interestingly, Dionysius of Alexandria had been a favorite pupil of Origen, and Origen a prized pupil of Clement of Alexandria; all three had been head of the Catechetical School there, Clement from 190 to 202, Origen for twenty-eight years, and Dionysius for fourteen.

In this he has many thoughts parallel to the Epistle to the Hebrews, and actually makes some verbal quotations from it showing clearly that it was not a recent production, and for this reason, too, it seemed natural to include it among the other writings of the Apostle. For Paul had spoken in writing to the Hebrews in their native language, and some say that the evangelist Luke, others that this same Clement translated the writing. And the truth of this would be supported by the similarity of style preserved by the Epistle of Clement and that to the Hebrews, and by the little difference between the thoughts in both writings.[8]

This comment by Eusebius appears in that section of the history in which he was citing the tradition about those who "first succeeded the Apostles, and were shepherds or evangelists in the churches throughout the world"[9]—Clement being named among them, along with Luke, and both Clement and Luke were understood to have been part of the Pauline circle. The view that Paul authored Hebrews was widely held among the Eastern churches, and Eusebius included quotes from many Eastern leaders about their views on that authorship.

In his reporting, Eusebius gave testimony that the Eastern church viewed Hebrews as both authoritative and apostolic because it was considered a Pauline writing. Eusebius knew, however, that some churches and leaders in the West did not view Hebrews as a Pauline work. Eusebius honestly reported the controversy because a part of his concern was to tell what the whole church had been saying "about the canonical and accepted Scriptures and what about those which are not such." As he wrote about all this, Eusebius had before him documents that had preserved the tradi-

---

8. *Ecclesiastical History*, Bk. III.xxxviii.1–3.
9. *Ecclesiastical History*, Bk. III.xxxvii.4.

tions honored in at least four major church centers of his day: Rome, Alexandria, Antioch, and Jerusalem.[10]

II. Hebrews in the New Testament Canon

It is important to note what was known and honored within the strategic church centers of the first and second centuries because, as we have seen, certain localities became prominent centers of tradition for faith and order. Those centers were also places where collections of authoritative documents were gathered and preserved and copied for use by local or even distant groups of believers. By examining and comparing those traditions, Eusebius traced how specific persons and writings were regarded and why that regard became fixed. Each region and church center tended to honor those writings which possessed "canonicity, or something like it, in a particular church for a particular period."[11] The major church centers in the East where a canonical tradition developed were Caesarea, Antioch, Alexandria, Ephesus, and Constantinople. The major church centers in the West to which the ancient writers referred in discussing canonical literature for the church were Rome, Carthage, and Lyons.[12]

The Greek term *kanon* means "measuring rod," a "bar" by which a standard measurement was determined. The word itself appears in four places in the New Testament literature, all within the Pauline letters: 2 Corinthians 10:13, 15, 16, and Galatians 6:16. In the first three uses, Paul

---

10. See the Introduction, Eusebius, *The Ecclesiastical History*, Vol. I, especially pp. xxxiii–xxxiv. See also J. B. Orchard, "Some Guidelines for the Interpretation of Eusebius' *Hist Eccl*. 3:34–39," in *The New Testament Age: Essays in Honor of Bo Reicke*, edited by William C. Weinrich (Macon, GA: Mercer University Press, 1984), Vol. 2, pp. 393–403.

11. Alexander Souter, *The Text and Canon of the New Testament* (London: Duckworth, 1912), p. 178.

12. Ibid., pp. 182–97. See also Brooke Foss Westcott, *A General Survey of the History of the Canon of the New Testament* (London: Macmillan and Co., 1881 fifth edition), especially pp. 337–50, 428–55.

was writing about the regulations he followed in handling his ministry, the rules under which he served as a preacher of the gospel. In his use of *kanon* in Galatians 6:16, Paul referred to what is normative for belief and behavior. By the second century, the term was widely used within the churches of the empire, and it denoted the basic faith of the Christian confession. Origen (c. 185–c. 254) was largely responsible for establishing this usage. By the fourth century, *kanon* was being used to denote the list of writings viewed as authoritative for stating the Christian faith and guiding the affairs of the church.

Those who referred to any certain writing as "canonical" had certain understandings about demands that writing met which could certify it as such: (1) distinct criteria were used to assess the writing as worthy of use for public worship; (2) an early date and use for that writing could be affirmed, backed by word from the closest church leader who could testify about its existence and use in certain places; and (3) solitary notices about the writing could be checked against more generally known references and uses of it.

The earliest listing of the books in our New Testament appeared in the Easter Letter written and sent by Athanasius, bishop of Alexandria (c. 296–373), to the clergy in his district in AD 367. As bishop, Athanasius was announcing the date of Easter for that year, and he purposely enumerated the writings that were authoritative for church use.[13] Still earlier, in preparing the Decrees of the Synod of Nicaea in c. 350, Athanasius had used the expression "not belonging to the canon" in discussing *The Shepherd of Hermas* document. One of the principal contributions Athanasius made to the church was to list those church writings that he and others considered canonical. Those he listed are the same twenty-seven writings we refer to as the New Testament. Later in that same fourth century, those

---

13. For an extract from the Thirty-Ninth Festal Letter of Athanasius, see Souter, *The Text and Canon of the New Testament* (London: Duckworth, 1912), Appendix E, pp. 213–17.

Preaching from Hebrews

same twenty-seven books were given special recognition as canonical by the clergy present at two general councils, namely the Council of Hippo in AD 393 and the all-African general council at Carthage in AD 412. The recognition by the councils of these selected church writings as canonical did not make them authoritative; that recognition only certified the already established place of authority these writings had within the church.

In singling out Hebrews as part of the canon, the fact that this letter was known before the close of the first century attests to its early appearance, and the fact that Clement of Rome quoted from it suggests its presumed use in Rome at an early date.

The Letter to the Hebrews appears in the oldest listing of the New Testament canon, usually associated with the writings of Paul.[14] The traditional ascription of Hebrews to Paul within the Eastern church secured a firm place for this writing within the New Testament. But it must not be overlooked that there was no common view among the church leaders in the East about how Paul was related to the writing. The tradition about Paul's exact responsibility as possible author of Hebrews was quite mixed and complex. The main question concerned the difference between the writing style in Paul's other letters as compared to that in Hebrews— Hebrews is written in refined Greek, while the known Pauline writings are

---

14. Hebrews has been positioned in many different orders within the letters of Paul. It is positioned between 2 Thessalonians and 1 Timothy in the Greek Codex Sinaiticus (4th cent.), Codex Vaticanus (4th cent.), Codex Alexandrinus (5th cent.), and Codex Ephraemi Rescriptus (5th Cent.). Other arrangements have been between Philippians and Philemon, after Philemon, after Titus, but always associated in some way with Paul's works. In the earliest papyrus manuscript of Hebrews (p. 46), usually dated c. AD 200, Hebrews is positioned between Romans and 1 Corinthians. On these different positionings, see Brooke Foss Westcott, *The Epistle to the Hebrews: The Greek Text with Notes and Essays* (Grand Rapids, MI: Wm. B. Eerdmans Publishing Co., 1980 reprint = 1892), pp. xxx–xxxii. See also W. H. P. Hatch, "The Position of Hebrews in the Canon of the New Testament," *Harvard Theological Review*, XXIX (1936), pp. 133–55.

not.[15] The churches in the West disputed Pauline authorship of Hebrews because of its *theology,* especially its teaching about the apparent impossibility of pardon for an apostate (see Heb 6:4–8). Interestingly, although the Letter to the Hebrews gained entrance into the canon on the strength of the Eastern tradition that Paul wrote or was behind its creation, the present positioning of Hebrews in our English versions places the letter *after* Paul's writings rather than *among* them. This order is based upon the Latin Vulgate, the translation work of the learned and noted Jerome (c. 345–c. 419), reputedly the ablest biblical scholar of the Western church at that time. The Latin Vulgate is a Western rendering that has had a primary influence upon our English Bible since it was the version on which the first English Bible was based. Although later English translations of the Bible have been made directly from the Hebrew, Aramaic, and Greek manuscripts rather than the Latin renderings, the order established for the books of the New Testament in the Latin Vulgate has continued as found there. Jerome was a scholar of the Western churches, and knowing the tradition within them of non-Pauline authorship of Hebrews, he placed this letter behind Paul's writings rather than in the midst of them. Jerome thus paid tribute to the tradition in place in the West regarding Hebrews, although he was personally influenced by the ancient Eastern tradition that Paul was responsible for writing the letter.

III. Authorship and Audience

The belief within the churches in the East that Paul the Apostle was responsible for Hebrews was ancient, as we have seen, but so were the

---

15. On the style of Hebrews, see Alexander Nairne, *The Epistle to the Hebrews* (Cambridge Greek Testament for Schools and Colleges) (Cambridge, England: Cambridge University Press, 1917), pp. cxlv–clxv; William Henry Simcox, *The Writers of the New Testament: Their Style and Characteristics* (Winona Lake, IN: Alpha Publications, 1980 reprint), pp. 39–59, 92ff.

questions about how he might have been responsible. Clement of Alexandria (c. 155–c. 200) suggested that Hebrews is Luke's polished Greek translation of a writing Paul originally made in Hebrew (or Aramaic), which would account for its difference in style from that apostle's other acknowledged writings. Eusebius gave the following report about Clement's views on this:

> And as for the Epistle to the Hebrews, he says indeed that it is Paul's, but that it was written for Hebrews in the Hebrew tongue, and that Luke, having carefully translated it, published it for the Greeks; hence, as a result of this translation, the same complexion of style is found in this Epistle and in the Acts but that the [words] "Paul an Apostle" were naturally not prefixed. For, says he, "in writing to Hebrews who had conceived a prejudice against him and were suspicious of him, he very wisely did not repel them at the beginning by putting his name."

Eusebius added:

> Then lower down he adds: "But now, as the blessed elder used to say, since the Lord, being the apostle of the Almighty, was sent to the Hebrews, Paul, through modesty, since he had been sent to the Gentiles, does not inscribe himself as an apostle of the Hebrews, both to give due deference to the Lord and because he wrote to the Hebrews out of his abundance, being a preacher and apostle of the Gentiles.[16]

Origen (c. 185–c. 254) also took note of the better Greek diction found in Hebrews and suggested that one of Paul's disciples or co-workers might

---

16. Eusebius, *Eccl. Hist.*, Bk. VI.xiv.2–4.

have prepared the letter from notes taken while Paul was teaching (or dictating). Eusebius quoted Origen's view as that scholar had stated it in his *Homilies* on Hebrews:

> Furthermore, he discusses the Epistle to the Hebrews, in his *Homilies* upon it: "That the character of the diction of the epistle entitled To the Hebrews has not the apostle's rudeness in speech, who confessed himself rude in speech, that is, in style, but that the epistle is better Greek in the framing of its diction, will be admitted by everyone who is able to discern differences in style. But again, on the other hand, that the thoughts of the epistle are admirable, and not inferior to the acknowledged writings of the apostle, to this also everyone will consent as true who has given attention to reading the apostle."

Eusebius continued:

> Further on, he adds the following remarks: "But as for myself, if I were to state my own opinion, I should say that the thoughts are the apostle's, but that the style and composition belong to one who called to mind the apostle's teachings and, as it were, made short notes of what his master said. If any church, therefore, holds this epistle as Paul's, let it be commended for this also. For not without reason have the men of old time handed it down as Paul's. But who wrote the epistle, in truth God knows. Yet the account which has reached us is twofold, some saying that Clement, who was the bishop of the Romans, wrote the epistle, others, that it was Luke, he who wrote the Gospel and the Acts.[17]

---

17. Ibid., Bk. VI. xxv.11–14.

Eusebius quoted a brief comment Dionysius of Alexandria (died c. 264) made about Hebrews. The comment was excerpted from a letter Dionysius wrote to Fabius, bishop of Antioch, commending the memory of those who had suffered martyrdom at Alexandria under Emperor Decius. Testifying about their steadfastness of faith, Dionysius likened them to "those of whom Paul testified, they took joyfully the spoiling of their possessions."[18] The words quoted in that tribute are from Hebrews 10:34, and Dionysius's ascription of them to Paul shows his view that Paul wrote Hebrews.

According to Tertullian (c. 155–c. 220), the noted apologist and theologian in the Western church, there was an equally ancient belief in the West that it was Barnabas, Paul's companion, who wrote Hebrews. In writing his treatise *On Modesty*, Tertullian quoted from Hebrews 6:1, 4–6 to make a point about discipline as an apostolic dogma and mentioned Barnabas as the writer.

> For there is extant withal an Epistle to the Hebrews under the name of Barnabas—a man sufficiently accredited by God, as being one whom Paul has stationed next to himself in the uninterrupted observance of abstinence."[19]

In his call to serious Christian living, Tertullian appealed to the strong witness of one who was part of the Pauline circle, and his attribution to Barnabas of that quotation from Hebrews shows his belief concerning who wrote it.

It is easy to understand how the view that Barnabas wrote Hebrews could make its way within certain of the churches. As a Levite, whose family, position, and work gave him an intimate knowledge of temple life, Barnabas had the background to treat the sustained argument about priestly

---

18. Ibid., Bk. VI.xli.6

19. Tertullian, "On Modesty," chapter XX, *The Ante-Nicene Fathers*, vol. 4, edited by Alexander Roberts and James Donaldson, (New York: Charles Scribner's Sons, 1925), p. 97.

ministry with which much of Hebrews deals. Hebrews ends, also, with the author describing his work as *logou tes parakleseos,* "a word of exhortation," (13:22), a description that reflects the style of preaching Barnabas and Paul did in synagogues (see Acts 13:15ff). Then too, Barnabas was known within the earliest Christian circles as a "Son of Encouragement" (Acts 4:36), a tributary sobriquet about his character and caring spirit.[20]

Ancient tradition in the Eastern church notwithstanding, the general consensus since the sixteenth century has been that Hebrews is a non-Pauline work. During the sixteenth century, a critical reassessment began among scholars studying the ancient traditions of the church; the conflicting views of the Eastern and Western sectors of the church were seriously studied, and other alternatives regarding the authorship of Hebrews were set forth and debated.[21] Major Greek scholars of that period expressed doubt that Paul wrote Hebrews, partly due to the recognizable differences between the Greek of his acknowledged writings and that found in Hebrews, and partly because of the restriction voiced in Hebrews 6:4–6 about non-forgiveness from God for apostates. Martin Luther (1483–1546) at first followed common custom in associating Hebrews with Paul, as his lectures on Hebrews during 1517–18 show. His view changed across the next decade, and his final consideration about who wrote the epistle is documented in a sermon he preached in 1537 on 1 Corinthians 3:4–5, a text in which Apollos is named: Luther commented about Apollos as "a highly intelligent man; the epistle of the Hebrews is certainly his."[22]

---

20. For an extended treatment of the case for Barnabas as author of Hebrews, see F. J. Badcock, *The Pauline Epistles: and the Epistle to the Hebrews in Their Historical Setting* (London: S.P.CK, 1937), especially pp. 183–84, 198–99.

21. For an excellent survey covering Hebrews research across most of the sixteenth century, see Kenneth Hagen, *Hebrews Commenting from Erasmus to Beze: 1516–1598* (Tuebingen, Germany: J. C. B. Mohr, 1981).

22. See Martin Luther, "Lectures on Titus, Philemon, and Hebrews," *Luther's Works,* vol. 29, edited by Jaroslav Pelikan (St. Louis: Concordia Publishing Co., 1968), especially pp. 109–241; Kenneth Hagen, *A Theology of Testament in the Young Luther: The Lectures*

The case against Paul's being the author of Hebrews is stronger than the case for his being its writer, although William Leonard wrote a strong defense in his favor.[23] Hebrews is pure Greek, and the writer's style is more florid than Paul, even considering the fact that Paul often used a secretary. Hebrews is filled with sentences with symmetry, euphony, and grand cadences (i.e., 1:1–4; 7:1–3), and effective word-groupings and sonorous compounds abound.[24] The way Hebrews quotes from the Old Testament is different from Paul's typical manner and even the version of the Old Testament differs from the version Paul used.[25] Then too, the writer's self-confession at Hebrews 2:3 that he was a second generation believer rules Paul out as the author.

Classical scholar William M. Ramsey (1851–1939) suggested in a 1908 study that Philip the Evangelist wrote Hebrews and that Paul endorsed the writing by adding the last verses.[26] Ramsey dated Hebrews between AD 55–57, written while Paul was imprisoned in Herod's palace in Caesarea (Acts 23:35). Philip the Evangelist had settled at Caesarea near the port (Acts 21:8), and he had continued a ministry there along with his four daughters.[27] Ramsey further suggested that Hebrews was initially sent

on Hebrews (Leiden, Netherlands: E. J. Brill, 1974), especially pp. 19–30; Martin Luther, Weimar edition of his works, vol. 45 (Weimar, Germany: Hermann Boehlau, 1911), p. 389.

23. See William Leonard, _The Authorship of the Epistle to the Hebrews_ (London: Burns, Oates, and Washbourne, 1939).

24. For the treatment of the Greek style and diction in Hebrews, see James Moffatt, _A Critical and Exegetical Commentary on the Epistle to the Hebrews_ (International Critical Commentary) (Edinburgh, Scotland: T. & T. Clark, 1924), especially pp. lvi–lxiv.

25. See E. Earle Ellis, _Paul's Use of the Old Testament_ (Grand Rapids, MI: Baker Book House, 1981), especially pp. 156–57,160–61, 170–71, 176–77,178–79, 187.

26. William M. Ramsey, _Luke the Physician: and Other Studies in the History of Religion_ (London: Hodder and Stoughton, 1908), see pp. 301–28.

27. Philip the Evangelist is to be distinguished from Philip the Apostle. The Evangelist was at first one of seven deacons of the church in Jerusalem (Acts 6:5) and was a Hellenist (Greek-speaking Jew), while Philip the Apostle was a Galilean (John 1:44) who probably used Palestinean-Aramaic mainly.

to the church in Jerusalem, the purpose being to reconcile parties there who held contending views about the meaning, merits, and promise of Judaism.

A few years earlier, in 1900, Adolf von Harnack (1851–1930) published a journal article in which he proposed that Priscilla wrote Hebrews, aided perhaps by her husband Aquila.[28] This, he suggested, would explain why there is no name attached to the letter as its author and why there is no opening paragraph of greeting, the fear being that prejudice against herself as a woman leader might hinder some within the Pauline churches from accepting her message. As for her leadership role, Harnack called attention to the fact that Priscilla (or Prisca, as Romans 16:2 names her, using the diminutive) is always named first when listed with her husband in New Testament records. She and her husband also knew Timothy, to whom reference is made in 13:23, the three having been intimates with Paul. Harnack also suggested that the pilgrimage motif in Hebrews might have been influenced by the travel associated with their work and that their craft as tentmakers was a natural backdrop for being sensitive to the tabernacle theme. Harnack's theorizing is problematic at more than one point, but especially at the point of the Greek wording at 11:32. There the writer asks rhetorically, "And what more shall I say? For time would fail me to tell of...." Although the personal pronoun *me* in that second sentence (11:32b) could be either masculine or feminine, the verb used there, "tell," *(diegoumenon,* "to narrate with fullness")* is a distinctly masculine participle in form. Harnack viewed this as a neutral use, but the masculine form argues against feminine authorship of Hebrews, unless Aquila played the dominant role in writing it.[29]

---

28. "Probabilia uber die Adreesse und den Verfasser des Hebraerbriefes," in *Zeitschrift: fur die Neutestamentliche Wissenschaft*, vol. 1 (1900), pp. 16–41.

29. For a recent feminist statement to reestablish the case for a woman writer of Hebrews, see Juliana Casey, *Hebrews* (Wilmington, DE: Michael Glazier,Inc., 1980), pp. xiii, xvii.

Charles P. Anderson has suggested more recently that Epaphras, a close companion of Paul, wrote Hebrews.[30] Epaphras was mentioned by Paul in Colossians (1:7; 4:12–13) as the chief worker in the Lycus Valley, where congregations had been established in Laodicea and Heirapolis. The suggestion also labels Hebrews as the letter "from Laodicea" to which Paul referred in Colossians 4:16, and the similarity of concern for Christian maturity in both Colossians (4:12) and Hebrews (5:14; 6:1; 9:9; 10:1, 14; 11:40; 12:2) is viewed as connectional. Robert Jewett, in his *Letter to Pilgrims,* a commentary on Hebrews, has agreed with Anderson, writing:

> Hebrews was written by Epaphras to the Lycus Valley situation at approximately the same time as Colossians was sent, which would be the winter of AD 55–56, according to my chronology of Paul's life.[31]

The "situation" referred to is explained as an incipient Jewish Christian gnosticism that threatened the apostolic message about the superiority of Jesus Christ over all angelic figures.

The name of Silas has been put forward as author of Hebrews, and so has that of Timothy.[32] The case for Silas as author has received strong support. According to Acts 15:22, Silas was one of the "leading men among the brethren" in the early church, and, like Paul, he was both a Hellenist

---

30. See Charles P. Anderson, "Who Wrote 'The Epistle From Laodicea'?" *Journal of Biblical Literature,* LXXXV (1966), pp. 436–40; idem., "The Epistle to the Hebrews and the Pauline Letter Collection," *Harvard Theological Review,* LIX (1966), pp. 429–438; idem., *Hebrews Among the Letters of Paul* (Studies in Religion), vol. V [1975–76], pp. 258–66.

31. Robert Jewett, *Letter to Pilgrims: A Commentary on the Epistle to the Hebrews* (New York: Pilgrim Press, 1981), p. 10.

32. On Timothy as possible author, see J. D. Legg, "Our Brother Timothy: A Suggested Solution to the Problem of the Authorship of the Epistle to the Hebrews," *Evangelical Quarterly,* vol. 40, (October–December, 1968), pp. 220–30. On Silas as the author, see E. G. Selwyn, *The First Epistle of Peter: The Greek Text with Introduction: Notes and Essays* (London: Macmillan & Co., Ltd., 1947, 2nd ed.), pp. 463–66. Thomas Hewitt also favors Silas as author in *The Epistle to the Hebrews: Introduction and Commentary* (London: Tyndale Press, 1960), pp. 29–32.

and a Roman citizen, as Acts 16:37 tells us. Silas was a chief missioner with Paul during the apostle's second missionary journey; he was well-known among the Pauline churches and an able co-partner within the Pauline circle. Silas was secretary (and perhaps joint-author) with Paul in writing to the Thessalonians (1 Thess 1:1; 2 Thess 1:1), and according to 1 Peter 5:12 (where his name is given as Silvanus, the Latin form of Hebrew Silas), he served as Peter's secretary in writing 1 Peter. But an even stronger case can be made for Silas as writer of Hebrews when the following factors are considered: Hebrews and 1 Peter have many strategic words in common and their doctrinal emphases agree in pointed detail; both letters reflect the same church problems; a setting of persecution is common to both works; the two writings give Old Testament passages the same focused treatment; and both Hebrews and 1 Peter were known at Rome at an early date.[33]

From among the many names put forward across the centuries as a suggested solution to the problem of who authored Hebrews, the greatest weight of "evidence" is on the side of Silas or Apollos, with a stronger probability that Apollos wrote the work.[34] Both Apollos and Silas were sometime members of the Pauline circle; both were Hellenized Jews and quite fluent in the Greek language.[35] According to Acts 18:24–28, Apollos was a second-generation Christian—as was the author of Hebrews (2:3),

---

33. According to 1 Peter 5:13, that epistle was written at "Babylon," the Christian code-name for Rome. See also the similar usage in the Revelation 14:8; 16:19; 17:5; 18:2, 10, 21.

34. See especially the strong statement for Apollos as writer that Ceslas Spicq has supplied, *L' Epitre aux Hebreux*, vol. 1 (Paris: J. Gabalda et Cie, 1952), pp. 197–219.

35. On the major members of the Pauline circle, see F. F. Bruce, *The Pauline Circle* (Grand Rapids, MI: Wm. B. Eerdmaus Publishiug Co., 1985). For Silas, see pp. 23–28; for Apollos, see pp. 51–57.

Acts 18:24–28 reports the background of Apollos. The *aner logios* in verses 24 is usually translated "an eloquent man," but it should be understood to include the sense of "cultured, learned." On Silas as a Hellenist, see E. G. Selwyn, *The First Epistle of Peter: The Greek Text with Introduction: Notes and Essays* (London: Macmillan & Co., Ltd., 1947, 2nd ed.), pp. 9–17.

but there is some question whether Silas was such. In 1 Thessalonians 2:7, Paul refers to himself and Silas (and Timothy?) as "apostles of Christ," a statement which might be viewed in a rather inclusive way since Silas was a sharer in apostolic mission, but it is possible that Silas was an apostle in his own right.[36] If this was so about Silas, or if he had himself heard Jesus during his earthy ministry, then Hebrews 2:3 would rule him out as writer of Hebrews.

Although no final word can be given yet about who wrote Hebrews, some factual statements can be made about its author:

1. The writer was a Hellenist by background and experience.

2. The writer was quite adept in the midrashic style.[37]

3. The writer was a master of rhetoric, with thought patterns marked by pointed imagery, wordplay, and dramatic vibrancy.

4. The writer was an experienced exegete and sermonizer.

5. The writer was familiar with Alexandrian thought and terminology, although it is not clear to what extent Platonic or Philonic views were purposely used in the general argument of Hebrews.[38]

---

36. On this, see E. G. Selwyn, *The First Epistle of Peter: The Greek Text with Introduction: Notes and Essays* (London: Macmillan & Co., Ltd., 1947, 2nd ed.), p. 11.

37. On midrash as a genre commonly used in the early Christian preaching, see Bo Reicke, "A Synopsis of Early Christian Preaching," in *The Root and the Vine: Essays in Biblical Theology*, written by Anton Fridrichsen and others (London: A. & C. Black, Ltd., 1953), p. 133. See also George Wesley Buchanan, *To the Hebrews: Translation, Comment and Conclusions* (The Anchor Bible) (Garden City, NJ: Doubleday & Co., 1976, 2nd ed.), pp. 246ff. 36.)

38. The debate continues over the extent to which the writer of Hebrews knew or was influenced by Alexandrian thought as represented in the works of Philo Judaens. The issue has been explored by many, but the following works are recommended: Sidney G. Sowers, *The Hermeneutics of Philo and Hebrews* (Zurich, Switzerland: Evz-Verlag, and Richmond, VA: John Knox Press, 1965); Ronald Williamson, *Philo and the Epistle to the Hebrews* (Leiden, Netherlands: E. J. Brill, 1970); Charles Carlston, "The Vocabulary of Perfection in Philo and Hebrews," in *Unity and Diversity in New Testament Theology: Essays in Honor of George E. Ladd*, edited by Robert A. Guelich (Grand Rapids, MI: Wm. B. Eerdmans Publishing Co., 1978), pp. 133–60.

6. The writer was more familiar with the Septuagint (LXX) text of the Old Testament than with the Hebrew text; the Greek alone was used.

7. The writer seems acquainted with Pauline thought but handled the kerygma with some independence,

8. The writer was a second-generation Christian (2:3).

9. The writer knew the people being addressed (5:11–12; 6:9–10; 10:32; 13:7, 19, 23).

10. The writer knew Timothy (13:23).

11. The writer completed and sent the letter before the destruction of Jerusalem.[39]

According to the New Testament description of Apollos, his personal traits and background match most, if not all, of the factors enumerated above. The Acts 18:24–28 passage introduces him as "a Jew" bearing the Latin name Apollonius (= Apollos), a "native of Alexandria," and "an eloquent man, well versed in the scriptures," with a passion for "showing by the scriptures that the Christ was Jesus." Interestingly, the Alexandrian church preserved no known account of any association between Apollos and the Letter to the Hebrews, but neither did that church preserve any mention of his connection with Paul. First Clement, written in Rome, mentions him, however, citing Apollos as "a man approved [*andri dedoki-masmeo*] by apostles.[40] Perhaps Priscilla and Aquila, his Christian tutors, had Apollos come to Rome and minister after they returned there following their years abroad as exiles due to the edict Emperor Claudius issued in AD 49–50 expelling all Jews from the capital city (see Acts 18:1–3).[41] By

---

39. If the author of Hebrews wrote after the destruction of the temple, mentioning that destruction would have strengthened his argument as found in chapters 7–10. See the treatment of this and other factors in John A. T. Robinson, *Redating the New Testament* (Philadelphia: Westminster Press, 1976), especially pp. 200–220.

40. First Clement, 47:4. See *The Apostolic Fathers*, vol. 1, trans. by Kirsopp Lake (Cambridge, MA: Harvard University Press, 1912), p. 91.

41 Suetonius, in his *Life of Claudius*, xxv.4, reported that "since the Jews constantly made disturbances at the instigation of Chrestus, he expelled them from Rome." It is

approximately AD 57, Priscilla and Aquila were back in Rome, leaders of a house-church assembly (Rom 16:3–5a), and, given their history of ministry together with Apollos in Corinth and elsewhere, they could well have introduced not only his name but even Apollos himself to believers there in Rome.

Mentioning the possibility that Apollos and the Christians in Rome knew each other is admittedly tenuous, since there is no clear evidence that they did, but mentioning that possibility is also necessary because the Hebrews letter reflects the author's knowledge of (or about) the godly leaders (apostolic figures?) who had nurtured their faith (2:3–4; 13:7), a knowledge of their background learning as Hebrews (6:1–2), an awareness that they were a closely knit fellowship (6:10; 10:24–25), and knowledge that some of them had suffered persecution and losses because they were ardent Christians (10:32–34).

The mention of Rome is also necessary, because of all the places suggested as the destination of the letter (Jerusalem, Corinth, Alexandria, Colossae, Ephesus, et al.), Rome best suits what seems indicated in the letter as the locale of its intended recipients.[42] The reference in 10:32 to the group's "hard struggle with suffering" could suggest either the time when Claudius exiled Jews from Rome (AD 49–50, several years after the Christian faith had taken root there) or the period of severity under Nero during the mid- to late-60s. Given the circumstance that further problems were

---

believed that the "disturbances" had to do with party struggles between Hebrew Christians who were zealous for Jesus as the Christ and those who resisted such teachings as anti-Judaic and heretical.

42. See, among many others, Ernest Findlay Scott, "The Epistle to the Hebrews and Roman Christianity," *Harvard Theological Review*, vol. 13 (1930), pp. 205–19; Gerhard Lenski, *The Interpretation of the Epistle to the Hebrews and the Epistle of James* (Columbus, OH: Wartburg Press, 1946), p. 22; William Manson, *The Epistle to the Hebrews: An Historical and Theological Reconsideration* (London: Hodder and Stoughton, 1951), pp. 171–72; See also Raymond E. Brown and John P. Meier, *Antioch and Rome: New Testament Cradles of Catholic Christianity* (New York: Paulist Press, 1983), especially pp. 142–51. See also Raymond E. Brown, *An Introduction to the New Testament* (New York: Doubleday, 1997), pp. 693–701.

anticipated (12:3–4, 7, 12–13), the author wrote to remind the believers about the meaning and guaranteed future of a maintained faith in Jesus (10:15–19; 13:6, 20–21).

Timothy, whom Paul had introduced to the church at Rome (Rom 16:21), had just been "set free" (Heb 13:23), presumably from imprisonment in or near the place of writing. The author shared this news, aware that those acquainted with Timothy would appreciate it. The author also shared greetings from those with him who were "from Italy" (Heb 13:24b), knowing that many would be encouraged by word from them. "Those from Italy" is usually taken as an indication that he was writing *to* Rome or to some place in Italy.[43] And since the author made no mention of the destruction of the temple in Jerusalem—an event that would have strengthened his argument—the Letter to the Hebrews should be dated probably after AD 64 but certainly before AD 70.[44]

Rome, the center of the empire, was the city of cities, even for a man like Paul whose Jewish heritage made Jerusalem, the Holy City, a treasured place in his heart. A great populace was active there. The metropolitan area was vast, the population was polyglot, and different ethnic and cultural groups existed side by side in diversity, social distance, and in spiritual need. Lucius Annaeus Seneca (54 BC–AD 39) in one of his *Moral Essays* wrote revealingly about how Rome's vast populace had changed the face

---

43. Raymond E. Brown has commented, "That the work was addressed to an Italian city other than Rome is implausible: It has to be a city with considerable Jewish Christian heritage and tendency, where Timothy is known, where the gospel was preached by eyewitnesses (2:3), and where the leaders died for the faith (13:7)—no other city in Italy would have matched all or most of those descriptions" (Raymond E. Brown and John P. Meier, *Antioch and Rome: New Testament Cradles of Catholic Christianity* [New York: Paulist Press, 1983], p. 146n313).

44. On the dating of Hebrews, see John A. T. Robinson, *Redating the New Testament* (Philadelphia: Westmiinster Press, 1976), pp. 200–220; F. F. Bruce, *The Epistle to the Hebrews* (Grand Rapids, MI: Wm. B Eerdmans Publishing Co., 1990, rev. ed.), especially pp. 20–22, 99n57; William L. Lane, *Hebrews 1–8* (Word Biblical Commentary) (Dallas: Word Books, 1991), pp. lxiii–lxvi.

of the city, lamenting, "Here reside more foreigners than natives."[45] "Have all of them summoned by name and ask of each: 'Whence do you hail?' You will find that there are more than half who have left their homes and come to this city, which is truly a very great and a very beautiful one, but not their own."[46]

Some of those foreigners were Jewish, but so were some of the natives. Aquila and Priscilla were known to have lived in Rome (Acts 18:2), part of a Jewish community that was there as early as 139 BC.[47] The Jews in Rome enjoyed a constituted freedom there. Helped by the influence of Herod the Great (47–4 BC), whom Caesar favored, Jews throughout the Diaspora organized their own community life, enjoyed religious freedom, and were exempt from military service.[48] Julius Caesar even permitted the Jews in Rome to send money back to Jerusalem to support the temple system. But there were times when Jews in Rome suffered from repressive measures, as in AD 19, and Suetonius reported about how Claudius expelled Jews from Rome in AD 49–50 (which Acts 18:2 reflects).[49]

Rome was home to many Jews, and the social differences their religious beliefs demanded was not usually a problem for the authorities. It is believed that Claudius rescinded religious toleration regarding Jews when social strain developed within Rome's Jewish community after Chris-

---

45. Seneca, *Moral Essays*, vol. 2, trans. by John W. Basore (Cambridge, MA: Harvard University Press, 1951 reprint = 1935), p. 431.

46. Ibid.

47. See E. Mary Smallwood, *The Jews Under Roman Rule: From Pompey to Diocletian* (Leiden, Netherlands: E. J. Brill, 1976), especially pp. 210–16. See also A. H. M. Jones, *The Cities of the Eastern Roman Provinces* (Oxford, England: Oxford University Press, 1971); Wolfgang Wiefel, "The Jewish Community in Ancient Rome and the Origins of Roman Christianity," in *The Romans Debate*, edited by Karl Paul Donfried (Minneapolis: Augsburg Publishing house, 1977), pp. 100–119.

48. See Emil Schurer, *The History of the Jewish People in the Age of Jesus Christ: 175 B.C.–A.D. 135),* vol. 3, revised and edited by Geza Vermes, Fergus Millar, and Martin Goodman, (Edinburgh, Scotland T. & T. Clark Ltd., 1973), especially pp. 73–81, 95–100.

49. See Suetonius, *Lives of the Caesars: Claudius* 25:4 (Loeb Classical Library) (Cambridge, MA: Harvard University Press, 1929), vol. 2, trans. by J. C. Rolfe.

tian Jews began aggressively evangelizing about Jesus as the Christ. As Suetonius reported it, "Since the Jews constantly made disturbances at the instigation of Chrestus, he [Claudius] expelled them from Rome." When Claudius died in AD 54, Jewish exiles returned to the city, but conflict between church and synagogue doubtless continued, and, in time, conflict between church and state. Historian E. Mary Smallwood has written:

> The recognition of Christianity as a religion distinct from
> and hostile to its parent Judaism seems to have been made
> in Rome by the 60s, but precisely when and how the Roman
> authorities made the distinction is not known.[50]

Whenever that distinction was made, the Christian Jews felt the brunt of its consequences, and the writer of Hebrews sent his letter to address the believers who were experiencing strain (10:32–39; 12:3–13, 28–29) and the temptation to return to radical Judaism so as to avoid economic pressures and property loss, since Mosaic Jews normally enjoyed legal standing.[51] The reference in Hebrews 10:32–34 states that some Christian Jews had experienced imprisonment. This letter anticipated further troubles, so it must have been written far enough after AD 49 for that earlier time of trouble under Claudius to be referred to as "those earlier days."

The title "To Hebrews" appears in all manuscripts of that letter, both papyrus and vellum, from at least the third century. Whether that title is original or was added by scribes to indicate the contents and presumed

---

50. E. Mary Smallwood, *The Jews Under Roman Rule: From Pompey to Diocletian* (Leiden, Netherlands: E. J. Brill, 1976), p. 217.

51. "A factor which remained almost completely constant was the political tolerance of the Jewish religion, and above all that freedom of movement without which the Jewish communities could not have developed a life of their own" (Emil Schurer, *The History of the Jewish People in the Age of Jesus Christ*: 175 B.C.–A.D. 135, vol. 3, revised and edited by Geza Vermes, Fergus Millar, and Martin Goodman [Edinburgh, Scotland T. & T. Clark Ltd., 1973], p. 114.

audience of the letter is not known, but no manuscripts of Hebrews have an alternative title.

Given the title of the letter, it is necessary to state that the particular Hebrews being addressed in this letter were Jews who had acknowledged Jesus as Lord (2:3). They not only knew "the basic teaching about Christ" (6:1) but they were part of a community with memories of the preaching and happenings associated with the active presence of one or more apostolic figures (2:3–4).[52] Some members of the community could be described as radical Hebrews: they were persons who regularly spoke Aramaic or Hebrew and were still influenced by Judaism's feasts, laws, circumcision, and so forth, even though they believed that Jesus is the Christ. Some other members could be described as relational Hebrews: they were Hellenists rooted in Greek culture, steeped in Judaism but using Greek as their daily language and the Septuagint (LXX) as their Bible. Acts 6:1 and 7:48–50 shed light on the distinction made here between the two classes of Hebrews who had become followers of Jesus. Given the elegant Greek used to write this letter and the fact that all of the Old Testament texts quoted in it are from the Septuagint (LXX) rather than the Hebrew text or Aramaic Targums, the author of Hebrews wrote with Hellenistic Jews in focus but with concern for the entire Christian community there in Rome.

IV. Argument and Outline of the Letter

Intent on helping his readers understand the meaning and significance of Jesus, the writer exhorted them to stop thinking in cultic terms and to stop trusting cultic forms, because through his death Jesus opened "the new and living way" (10:20), which grants believers an "eternal redemp-

---

52. Concerning the "attestations" enumerated in 2:3–4 see Charles Kingsley Barrett, *The Signs of an Apostle* (London: Epworth Press, 1970).

tion" (912). He reported that the old covenant offered to Jews has been superseded by a new one offered to all people (Heb 10:16–18 = Jer. 31:33, 34b). He reminded them of Jesus' status as God's Son (1:1–2; 4:14)), the promised Christ (3:6, 14), and he interpreted passages in the Hebrew Scriptures that announce his person and work. Thoroughly informed by both the Hebrew Scriptures and the apostolic message, the writer explained that the old covenant regimen of animal sacrifices represented and foreshadowed the offering Jesus made to God of himself, and he urged the readers to understand that by that deed all believers are "sanctified through the offering of the body of Jesus Christ once for all" (10:10). Because of this, animal sacrifices are no longer necessary, nor the priesthood that administered them. This Christ-centered hermeneutic is fully in line with the apostolic teaching they had heard and known, and the writer warned that forsaking Jesus to trust in an obsolete ritualistic order was to commit apostasy (6:4–6; 10:26–31).

The readers were exhorted, therefore, to "pay greater attention to what we have heard" (2:1) because it "was attested to us by those who heard [the Lord]" (2:3). They were advised to "consider" (3:1; 12:3), to "take care" (3:12), to "exhort one another" (3:13), to hold their confidence "firm" (3:14), to hold fast to their "confession" (4:14; 10:23). They were instructed to "recall" and "remember" (10:32), and urged to "go on toward perfection" (6:1), to show "diligence" (6:11), and to maintain faith (10:39). They were exhorted to "lay aside every weight and the sin that clings so closely" (12:1), to "run with perseverance" (12:1), to look steadily to Jesus (12:2), and to pursue peace with everyone (12:14). They were to continue exercising mutual love (13:1) and to remain free from "love of money" (13:5). Some persons had already abandoned the fellowship (10:25), and the writer cautioned the rest against neglecting to assemble. The conditions the group faced demanded such instruction, and the writer sent it in an encouraging letter flavored with the evident caring of a pastoral heart.

The Letter to the Hebrews is a dynamic restatement of the Christian faith. The message is in a sequence that reminds, informs, illuminates, warns, encourages, and challenges. The structural pattern of Hebrews is unique among the New Testament writings. Unlike the Pauline letters, which are mainly twofold in structure, with one extensive doctrinal section followed by an application section, Hebrews has several sections in which doctrinal segments alternate with exhortational application sections:

Teaching Statement	Application
1:1–14	
	2:1–4
2:5–3:6a	
	3:6b–4:16
5:1–10	
	5:11–6:20
7:1–10:18	
	10:19–13:25

Viewed thematically, however, the letter may be outlined as follows:

Introduction: A Doctrinal Manifesto about Jesus (1:1-4)
I. God's Son as His Supreme Agent (1:5–4:13)
   A.   Superiority of the Son over Angels (1:5–2:18)

1. The Son's Relation to God (1:5–14)

2. Exhortation Based on the Contrast (2:1–4)

3. The Son's Relation to Believers (2:5–18)

B. Superiority of the Son over Moses and Joshua (3:1–4:13)

1. The Son Greater than Servants in the Household (3:1–6)

2. Exhortation Based on the Contrast (3:7 –19)

3. The "Rest of God" Explained (4:1–10)

4. Exhortation to Full Obedience (4:11–13)

II. *Jesus the Great High Priest (4:14–10:39)*

A. The Priesthood of Jesus Introduced (4:14–10:39)

1. The High Priestly Ministry Explained (5:1–4)

2. Jesus as Divinely Appointed High Priest (5:5–10)

3. Exhortation to Become Mature (5:11–6:3)

4. The Awesome Problem of Apostasy (6:4–8)

5. A Call to Diligence in Faith and Service (6:9–12)

6. The Surety of Hope Set on Jesus (6:13–20)

B. Melchizedek as Type of the Son's Priesthood (7:1–28)

1. Melchizedek Preceded Levitical Priesthood (7:1–10)

2. Imperfections of the Levitical Order (7:11–19)

3. The Perfection of Jesus as High Priest (7:20–28)

C. The Old Covenant Contrasted with the New One (8:1–13)

D. The Earthly Sanctuary Contrasted with the Heavenly One (9:1–28)

E. Animal Sacrifices Contrasted with Jesus' Death (10:1–18)

1. Animal Sacrifices as a "Shadow" (10:1–4)

2. Jesus' Offering of Himself Brings Reality (10:5–18)

F. Exhortation to Gain Real Access to God (10:19–31)

G. Exhortation to Faith and Perseverance (10:32–39)

III. The Meaning and Necessity of Faith (11:1–12:29)

    A.   Faith Defined (11:1–3)

    B.   Faith Illustrated (11:4–40)

    C.   Faith and Disciplined Living (12:1–11)

    D.   Exhortation to Steadfastness in Faith (12:12–17)

    E.   The Privileged Position of the Believer (12:18–29)

IV. Concluding Remarks (13:1–25)

    A.   Christian Relationships (13:1–6)

    B.   Christian Duties (13:7–17)

    C.   Personal Expressions (13:18–25)

Chapter 2

Unit Reflections

Introduction: A Doctrinal Manifesto about Jesus (1:1–4)

1:1–4. The Letter to the Hebrews begins on a high note, with a doctrinal manifesto about Jesus as God's Son and supreme agent of ministry. The writer's beginning statement is a beautifully worded periodic sentence in Greek, but modem translators usually break that single sentence into shorter ones for easier reading (as, for example, the three-sentence format in the New Revised Standard Version and in the New English Bible). The contrast in verses 1–2 between God's prophetic servants and his Son, Jesus (first named at 2:9), should be readily understood. The prophets were all limited by their humanity and historical circumstances, while the Son speaks of his Father with a full inside view of the divine will. There is thus a fullness and finality to what the Son has said, and there is an ultimacy to what he as Son has done.

Next, in verses 3–4, all that the Son has done to make a complete "cleansing for sins" is mentioned, and his holy character and exalted status are celebrated as evidences for his sufficiency. Thus, to be seated now "at the right hand of the Majestic One on high" is both his privilege and his due. But the "sitting" suggests more: It suggests that the work he set out to do has been done and that his work stands worthily completed. His sitting with God implies both a responsibility now completed and his first estate restored. Obtaining "a more excellent honor," or "name," than any of the angels implies that God rewarded the Son for his excellent but costly ministry as the promised Suffering Servant.

I. God's Son as His Supreme Agent (1:1—4:13)

A. Superiority of the Son over Angels (1:5-2:18)

1. THE SON'S RELATION TO GOD (1:5-14)

1:5–14. After the lofty doctrinal pronouncement about Jesus as Son of God, the writer then proceeds to document the Son's superior status over angels by calling into use selected texts from the Hebrew Scriptures. Some of the texts he used are viewed as words spoken by God *to* the Son (1:5 quotes Ps 2:7; 2 Sam 7:14; and 1 Chron 17:13; vv 8–9 quote Ps 45:6–7; vv 10–12 quote Ps 102:25–27, and v 13 quotes Ps 11:01). Some other texts are viewed as words spoken by God *about* the Son, with angels being addressed (v 6 quotes Deut 32:43).

The writer's use of Psalm 2:7 as God's utterance to the Son reflects the understanding of the early church about the God-bestowed kingship that Jesus holds. This psalm was one of many that were viewed as Messianic in import. Originally part of a coronation liturgy from the time of David the King, the wording of the psalm reports God's pleasure with the one being installed as king over the nation. Here in Hebrews, that commendation is cited in tribute to Jesus as the kingly Son; it is an acclamation of his worthiness to receive honor and to be obeyed. The early church did so honor him, and Psalm texts were among the lively tributes utilized in worship settings as well as in church writings such as this epistle.

The citation of Psalm 45:6–7 in verses 8–9 points to the supreme virtue of Jesus as the One who always honored the will of God in his decisions and deeds: "You have loved righteousness and hated evil." The word "righteousness" will appear six times in this letter (1:9; 5:13; 7:2; 11:7, 33; 12:11), and later, in 5:13–14, the writer will make an appeal to his readers to develop character within that righteousness, so that by moral discernment and a love for what is right, genuine spiritual growth can steadily take place in their lives.

In verses 10–12, Psalm 102:25–27 is quoted, and this was probably to emphasize the eternality of the Son over against the changing patterns and systems of human history. The faithful are being reminded that they are secure through the unfailing ministry of an eternal, unchanging Lord. This emphasis will again be in view at 13:8, where the writer proclaims that "Jesus Christ is the same yesterday, and today, and throughout the ages."

2. EXHORTATION BASED ON THE CONTRAST BETWEEN JESUS AND ANGELS (2:1–4)

2:1–4 The "therefore" in 2:1 introduces an important conclusion to the writer's statement about the status of Jesus. We must give serious attention to him—or suffer the sad consequences for failing to do so. Although angels have been sent as "servant spirits," intimately involved in human ventures, God has backed their word and work, punishing all who refused to honor what those servant spirits were sent to accomplish. The word Jesus has given is the ultimate and final word from God, and is therefore indispensable. It is the word about salvation, and in its richest dimensions, a salvation brought into effect and fully guaranteed only for those who seriously listen to Jesus and look to him with right understanding about who he is. The exhortation is a warning about what is lost by those who, having heard the message about salvation, selfishly and faithlessly "drift away [from it]."

3. THE SON'S RELATION TO BELIEVERS (2:5–18)

2:5–18 Having completed his preliminary statement about the superiority of Jesus over angels, and having issued a warning not to be part of the awesome fate of those who neglect the witness and work provided by the Son of God, the writer moves on in 2:5–18 to begin a discussion about how the Son stands related to those who do believe on him.

In this section of Hebrews we get our first insight from the writer about the extent to which Jesus as Son fully identifies with our humanity and its attendant experiences. Like the first humans, Jesus lived for a while "lower [in condition] than angels" (2:9), but unlike them he never failed the high purpose for which he entered the world. He too had to live by faith, by a steady trust in God as he lived his way across the years. The writer documents the Son's need for faith by quoting Isaiah 8:17b, using it at 2:13 as a confessional word from the Son about his life under God—"I [myself] will firmly trust in him." The writer thus accents attention upon Jesus as religious *subject* in order to highlight the importance of Jesus as religious *object*. In so doing, the writer's insight into the human experience of Jesus accents his obedience in pilgrimage; it shows him as a figure of hope for those who look to him as the worthy "pioneer of their deliverance" (2:10). In looking to Jesus, the writer asserts, we can maintain our bearings, discern our possibilities, and anticipate our future. That future will ultimately involve life within another order which God has planned for his people: thus the expression "the coming world [order]" (2:5), a world (Gk. *oikoumene,* "inhabited, ordered community") under the manifest lordship of Jesus as exalted Son, now raised above the present world order and "crowned with glory and honor because of the [particular] death he suffered" (2:9). The sovereignty humans lost by sinning stands modeled in him in his victory over temptation, sin, and death. Jesus now heads the household of the faithful who will inherit the new order when this old earth order passes away.

What Jesus accomplished benefits all who identify with him. Jesus was a "pioneer" in our interest, intent to lead "many sons to glory" by his delivering deed of salvation. The "many sons" are, with him, full members of the very family of God. This was the concern of the incarnation. Jesus wanted to identify fully with humans in our plight, even becoming subject to death, so that he could make death itself his victim—from *inside* the experience. According to 2:14–16, the grand result for believers is release from the fear of death. Angels did not need such help; humans did, and Jesus eagerly made that help available.

At 2:17–18, the high priesthood theme is introduced to highlight further the great ministry of Jesus to believers. It is the theme the writer will continue to unfold and accent across the bulk of the letter. It is the rather extended treatment of this theme, together with the many details connected with the Day of Atonement ritual, which provides grounds for viewing this writing as written to and for Hebrews. (This letter is the only New Testament writing that explains the ministry of Jesus in terms of a high priesthood.) As one who suffered the round of human experience, Jesus can represent us well since he understands and identifies with our needs; he is before us as a victorious winner and with us as a sympathetic and strategic helper. The believer need only cry out for his assistance.

B. Superiority of the Son over Moses and Joshua (3:1–4:13)

1. THE SON GREATER THAN SERVANTS IN THE HOUSEHOLD (3:1–6)

3:1–6 Having set forth the high rank and great ministry of Jesus on behalf of his people, the writer issues an exhortation "consider Jesus." That word "consider" (Gk. *katanoesate*) was a call to fix the mind and heart upon him. The titles that follow increase the weight of his exampleship and importance for the believer. Jesus is "apostle" and "high priest" of our confession. This introduces a planned comparison between Jesus and Moses, the point being to show that Jesus has a superior ministry to that of Moses. Although both Moses and Jesus held appointments from God, were faithful to their calling, were deliverers of their people, established covenants, were suffering servants, and had face-to-face dealings with God, the ministry of Jesus was superior because he is Son, while Moses was but a servant within the household of God. The confession of the church centers in Jesus, who is God's superior messenger ("apostle") and the perfect representative of the needy people ("high priest"). In both instances of service, Jesus acts on behalf of others. Thus, however great others have been in their service for God, Jesus is worthy of greater honor. Problems abound when Jesus is not properly "considered," when his personhood and ministry are not kept in proper focus. As Son, Jesus presides over the "house[hold] of God" (3:5–6). The belonging is conditional: it happens through faith and steady "confidence and pride in our hope." A right pride in belonging stimulates faithfulness to the family name and leadership.

2. Exhortation Based on the Contrast (3:7–19)

3:7–19 The second warning section of the letter begins at 3:7–4:2. This section recalls Israel's failure in the wilderness, and the sad consequences of that failure by a people called by God to live as his nation.

The writer quotes Psalm 95:7–11 as he reported God's displeasure with the generation that provoked him by its waywardness and sin. It was a generation that lacked a listening ear for God's word. That generation was united in a shared sin, and its members fell in a shared fate. God let them succeed at sinning, but the gains were fleshly and destructive. The gains of sin are always deadly, making the disobedient losers. God had offered them "rest," but their sinning blocked the benefits of the offer.

3. The "Rest of God" Explained (4:1–10)

4:1–10 The privilege God offered the earlier generation still remains open. The promise God originally made still holds: one can "enter God's rest." Our period of time does not make us "come short" (Gk. *husterekenai,* "arrive too late") of it because the promise about "rest" involved something more than settling peacefully in the geographical spot called Canaan. The "good news" about rest involves more than a promised land; it involves a promised life in the will of God. The levels of fulfillment in the promise begin to be experienced when the promise meets with "faith in [on the part of] the hearer." Israel first heard the promise, which included cessation of warfare after victory over the enemies blocking their entrance into Canaan, but that generation did not even enter Canaan "because of unbelief" (3:19). God was not obligated to bless those who resisted his terms, but neither was he so displeased that he withdrew the offer of rest. A future realization was implied in the promise, and at the highest level of fulfillment. Possessing Canaan was not all that God had in mind for ancient Israel, and salvation here and now is not all that God has planned for believers now, the writer explains. The people of God will enjoy a coming "Sabbath Rest" at the dawning of "another day" (4:8b), the reference here being to the ultimate life with God.

4. EXHORTATION TO FULL OBEDIENCE (4:11–13)

4:11–13 "Let us be eagerly diligent (Gk. *spoudazo,* "concentrate with eager interest to succeed"), therefore, to enter into that rest."

A full striving will mean staying open toward God in heart and mind, with eagerness to hear his word in order to know and do his will. The reference in 4:12–13 to "the word of God" as a confronting sword no doubt recalls the encounter Joshua experienced with the angelic commander of the Lord's forces just before his attack upon Jericho (Josh 5:13–15). When Joshua realized that he was confronted by the Lord's angelic messenger, he fell submissively before him, listening for instructions. The writer here appeals to his readers to take the listening posture before the word of God. Openness to that word keeps one on good terms with God, to whom all are unavoidably accountable.

II. Jesus the Great High Priest (4:14—10:39)

A. The Priesthood of Jesus Introduced (4:14–16)

4:14–16 His life on earth now done, his mission here accomplished, Jesus has "passed into heaven," where he now ministers on our behalf before God, representing us as "the great high priest" at "the throne of grace, so that we may receive mercy and obtain grace for timely help when in need" (4:16). The believer has every encouragement, then, to remain faithful and trusting as members of God's household; there is a definite belonging and access to blessing from God. Prayer is offered to One who responds graciously, and there is an attitude of mercy that the believer meets when help is sought through prayer.

1. THE HIGH PRIESTLY MINISTRY EXPLAINED (5:1–4)

5:1–4 This section begins an extended discussion of the high priesthood of Jesus. First mentioned at 2:17, then restated at 3:1 and 4:14·, this title and theme of the Son's high priesthood is now expanded in 5:1–6:20 of the letter.

Recalling Exodus 28–29, where consecration for the priesthood is treated, the writer enumerates some of the qualifications necessary for someone to attain and hold the priestly role. The person must be "chosen from among men," actually from Aaron's lineage, "appointed to act on their behalf" in matters relating to God, primarily through the offering of "gifts and sacrifices for sin." The priest was not someone in general but someone in particular, divinely set apart for a distinctive service.

2. JESUS AS DIVINELY APPOINTED HIGH PRIEST (5:5–10)

5:5–10 Jesus answers every requirement for the priesthood, except one: he was not from Aaron's line. Yet he supersedes the Aaronic priesthood because he holds an eternal appointment "after the order of Melchizedek" (5:6, 10; 6:20; 7:11, 15, 17). This is a more distinctive priesthood because Melchizedek was the first priest mentioned in Israel's history, one whose importance was not granted by human descent but by divine decree, a fact testified when Abraham offered tithes to him. The priesthood associated with Aaron and his descendants was a later and more limited order than that accorded by God to Melchizedek. The role of the Aaronic priesthood constantly passed on from one priest to another because each priest died, while the priestly ministry of Jesus continues unchanged because it is eternal, unaffected by the passage of time because "he always lives," standing before God on our behalf. His place of privilege remains his by divine right, but it was gained by his obedience to the terms of sonship. Now successful through his pilgrimage in the world, Jesus has become "the source of eternal salvation to all those who obey him" (5:9).

3. EXHORTATION TO BECOME MATURE IN UNDERSTANDING (5:11–6:3)

5:11–6:3 The truth about Jesus as high priest is a great truth that demands a mature understanding and appreciation. Those who are spiritually sluggish and "dull of hearing" (5:11) miss the depth of meaning this truth holds for their lives. Thus the writer's third warning passage. He chided the readers to move from a child's diet of milk to the solid food of righteousness that would prepare them for the rigors of life believers face. He wanted them to learn how to endure stress in the spirit and manner Jesus exemplified during "the days of his flesh" (5:7). The readers needed to become "mature," trained by practice to distinguish good from evil (5:14). Maturity in faith depends upon the same logic as does any other growth: one must advance stage by stage and not be forever preoccupied with beginning anew. As in the natural, so in the spiritual, the key to proper nurture is appetite and the will to advance.

The writer thus advised "Let our movement be toward maturity" (6:1). He was eager to stimulate the spiritual appetite of his readers for the deeper truths about the person and ministry of Jesus. He hoped to leave behind, without mention, the foundational teachings with which they were presumably familiar (i.e., the meaning of repentance, how baptism differs from other ceremonial washings, the ritual import of laying on of hands, the resurrection hope, and the expectation of a final judgment) (6:1b–2). But as he reflected further on the foundational matters, his covenantal concern stirred the writer to voice another warning. The warning this time is about the possible irremediable loss of salvation through apostasy.

4. THE AWESOME PROBLEM OF APOSTASY (6:4–8)

6:4–18 Although there is great danger involved in any sinning, the deed of apostasy is more devastatingly dangerous. The tragedy of apostasy is that one steps aside from the truth deliberately, with a full change of mind about it all, and with an offensive attitude toward what one once embraced as worthy of trust. Only someone who has once believed can be guilty of such a sin, which shows the spirit of rejection where faith once motivated them.

Hebrews 6:4–8 (and the similar passage at 10:26–31) must be understood as the writer's pastoral concern for his readers. The warning was against "apostasy" (Gk. *parapipto*, "to step aside deliberately"). The message here is that there must be no change of mind about the faith after one has experienced its realities and effects. No faulty or offensive attitude against the faith must be allowed to develop. There should be no loss of hope, no matter how long God takes to meet one's expectations (6:11–12). Devotion and diligence demand each other, and they indelibly mark the true disciple of the Lord.

Hebrews 6:4–8 has been a problem passage across many centuries of church life. The writer's statement that "it is not possible to restore to repentance those who...have fallen away" (6:4a, 6a) has been understood in different ways: (1) that there is no second forgiveness for backsliders; (2) that there are limitations to God's forgiveness; (3) that this is a supposed situation in order to instruct believers to remain serious and growing in their faith; and (4) that this is a real situation that can happen to someone who has known the benefits of salvation. The wording is rather rigorous and suggests that the former believer has now changed his or her mind about following Jesus, presumably to save themselves from some situation of outward threat. Hebrews 10:26 sheds a bit more light on the matter with its wording about "sinning deliberately," implying an attitude of contempt for what one once embraced; 10:27 classifies the one who is guilty of apostasy as being an "adversary" (Gk. *hupenantios,* "willfully set against"), while 6:6 pictorially classifies such a one as crucifying the Son of God on their own, "exposing him to public ridicule." Only a former believer can be apostate, but this kind of sinning is not the same in effect as lapsing or backsliding. The writer plainly warns his readers, eager that each and all avoid that selfishness of soul that becomes prelude to the radical renunciation of Christ.

5. A CALL TO DILIGENCE IN FAITH AND SERVICE (6:9–12)

6:9–12 Building on the parable he has introduced, which reminds that farmers give tender attention to land that responds well to cultivation but burn away the thorns and thistles from land that produces undesirable growth, the writer quickly registers his expectation that his readers want to be like good growth on richly productive land. Unlike undesirable growth, true and faithful believers need not fear judgment but continuing care from God.

6. THE SURETY OF THE HOPE SET ON JESUS (6:13–20)

6:13–20 Waiting is not easy for humans who are eager for the completion or correction of things in their lives. Even waiting on God can be an experience of strain, a testing factor, an unsettling burden—except for those who set themselves to become strong, steadied, and calmed by patience. Patience is expected on the part of believers because the promises of God are always sure. The entire civilized world honors oath-making as part of a valid contract. The more serious the contract, the more distinct the means for confirming it. Thus God's oath to confirm his promise to us.

The Christian hope is based on the sure promises of God to his people. That hope is for us what an anchor is for a ship—it is a steadying factor, a tie with the depths. Actually, however, our real tie is not below but above, in the heights, "where Jesus has gone as a forerunner on our behalf" (6:20). Jesus has not only gone ahead of us into the presence of God, as our "forerunner" *(prodromos,* "advance agent"), but he has left trailing evidence about the direction we should follow to join him there.

B. Melchizedek as Type of the Son's Priesthood (7:1–28)

This section of the Hebrews letter details how the two priestly orders differed and why the "order of Melchizedek" was superior to that of Aaron. But if the question is raised about why so much attention is being devoted to the priesthood theme in this letter, the answer can be quickly given. The religious life of the Hebrews was centered in the sacrificial worship and only priests were divinely authorized to offer prescribed sacrifices. The religious duties of the faithful demanded the services of a priest above those of any other community leader. The priesthood was a special classification and community within a community; its boundaries were established by divine order and membership in the priestly caste was restricted to the one family line of Aaron (Ex 29:9b, "and the priesthood shall be theirs by a perpetual statute").

In Hebrews 7, the writer explains that even the sanctioned priesthood has severe limitations despite its high purpose: (1) its service could not grant anyone full access to God (7:11); (2) it operated on the basis of a severely restricting set of laws (7:18); (3) it involved a succession of persons who could not continue in office because each one died and had to be replaced by someone new (7:23); (4) every Aaronic priest was a sinner and thus needed to have his own sins handled before being able to assist others by his work (7:27); and (5) God had announced earlier a plan to supersede the Aaronic priesthood at an appointed time and that the new priest would be like the legendary Melchizedek, whose priesthood was earlier than Aaron's and not limited by the factor of family lineage (7:15–17). Thus the detailed discussion about Melchizedek as superior to Aaron and his line.

1. MELCHIZEDEK PRECEDED LEVITICAL PRIESTHOOD (7:1–10)

7:1–10 Melchizedek was a king-priest, a unique appointee under God, and one whose service-role was not passed on to someone else. Jesus is "like Melchizedek" in these respects, and "remains a priest for ever." No succession is necessary—or possible. Succession was inevitable among the Levitical priests because each one died in time, leaving the work to be handled by yet another apprentice. Each one "received the priestly office" under strict terms of lineage, physical readiness, and anointing; but each one yielded that office under the common demand of death. Each one was great, as to task, and responsible, as to trust, receiving tithes. But a greater priest than all the others was promised, has come, and continues, one "like Melchizedek" but who is the Son of God.

The discussion turns upon two Old Testament passages: Genesis 14:18–20 and Psalm 110:4, which are the only two references to the ancient biblical literature about the life and work of Melchizedek. Despite the brevity of material about the man, a considerable tradition regarding Melchizedek had developed in Hebrew thought across the centuries. Psalm 110:4 reflects some of that thought about his importance as a priestly type. The writer of Hebrews claims that Psalm 110:4 points beyond Melchizedek to Jesus; his interest is not in Me1chizedek alone but in what that first priest represents as a type, namely: (1) an earlier order of priesthood than that of Aaron; (2) an eternal ministry—he has "neither date of birth nor date of death…and remains a priest perpetually" (7:3); (3) someone external to Aaron's family line; and (4) his ministry is based on direct appointment by God—"Thou art a priest forever" (7:21c). The One about whom these things speak most fully, the writer claims, is Jesus.

Unit Reflections   **61**

2. Imperfections of the Levitical Order (7:11–19)

7:11–19 There was a restricting temporariness about the Levitical priesthood and the legal system under which that order operated. Now, in Jesus, that weak and limited system for dealing with sin has been superseded by the life and ministry of One who has an "indestructible life." It was all foretold in that prophetic word in Psalm 110:4. The writer quotes that word, which is a divine decree, and announces that the reference is to Jesus—another kind of priest, hailing from another tribe, holding a higher rank, and the guarantor of a new and better covenant. The human need is fully met in such a new priest, by whose life and ministry we now have "a better hope, through which we [do] draw near to God" (7:19).

3. The Character and Perfection of Jesus as High Priest (7:20–28)

7:20–28 Jesus holds a priesthood that will not change, and it holds no limitations in its effects. A new covenant (Gk. *diatheke,* "arrangement, settlement") is now operative, one that assures believers of a full acceptance by God because Jesus, his Priest-Son, is our Advocate and ally. As the holy One, Jesus is pure enough to help us. As the heavenly One, he is powerful enough to help us. But also human, with us, he is related enough to help us.

C. The Old Covenant Contrasted With the New One (8:1–13)

8:1–13 After his strategic statement about the superlative character of Jesus as the eternal high priest (7:26–28), the writer offers a summary word about the high priesthood theme in 8:1–6 and then moves ahead to develop his argument about the new covenant now in effect through the sacrificial deed of his death (chaps 8–10).

Chapter 8 begins the central section of the Hebrews letter. It is the section in which the writer contrasts the old order and the new, and he does so with three aspects in view: (1) covenant benefits; (2) sanctuary matters; and (3) the nature of the sacrifice demanded. The line of thought is quite detailed, demanding familiarity with the Jewish way of worship as reported in the Old Testament. An additional difficulty in the writer's argument is his use of imagery: shadow *(skia,* 8:5) as contrasted with reality *(alethinos,* "true," 8:2), copy *(hupodeigma,* 8:5) in relation to pattern *(tupos,* 8:5), and "earthly" in contrast to what is "heavenly." According to his argument Jesus is now ministering in "that true tabernacle which the Lord himself erected, not man" (8:2); the earthly sanctuary that the workers had to take down and set up again every time the nation moved about during the wilderness years was the "shadow of the heavenly reality" (8:5). The full contrast between the earthly and heavenly finally involves the difference between "the blood of goats and bulls" and "the blood of Christ" (9:12–14), the benefit of the latter being "eternal redemption" for true believers. The analogies, contrasts, and comparisons in this section of the Hebrews letter are part of the writer's attempt to demonstrate the meaning of the eternal ministry of Jesus as the new "high priest…seated at the right hand of the throne of the Majestic One in the heavens" (8:1). Given this real, effective, and sufficient ministry for us on his part, there is no further need for what earthly priests do in temples made with hands. The promised period of time documented in Jeremiah's prophecy about the true binding of the human soul with God's clear will is *focused present* in Hebrews. True believers can now go beyond the limitations of ritual to experience what is real. The old covenant is now obsolete, dismissed to make room for the new order effected by the priestly Son of God.

D. The Earthly Sanctuary Contrasted with the Heavenly One (9:1–28)

9:1–28 Chapter 9 opens with a description of the covenantal regulations for worship and how the floor plan of the tabernacle (Gk. *skene,* "tent") was to be symbolic for teaching about spiritual matters. The place of worship had stipulated furniture (e.g., lamp stand , table, golden altar of incense, ark of the covenant), all of which was emblematic as well as historical. Aware that some of his readers might need a further description of the full meaning of these pieces of furniture, the writer issued a demurrer as he proceeded, stating that he could not treat everything in detail: "about which there is no time now to treat in detail" (9:5b). He was intent on treating the *point* for mentioning that earthly sanctuary, namely that it represented something more than itself, that it was all "a parable of the present time" (9:9).

The earthly tabernacle was but a "copy" of the real or "heavenly," where God dwells; the inner Holy Place was restricted to all except the high priest, and he could enter it "only once a year" (9:7), and even the sacrifices he was commissioned to offer on behalf of the sinning people were of limited effect because they could not "bring the worshipers to perfection with respect to conscience" (9:9). With the mention of "conscience" (Gk. *suneidesis,* consciousness, a relational knowledge), the writer has called into clear view the one real human need for which the old sacrificial system was inadequate. The offering of sacrificial animals could not secure a lasting redemption for the people. The ritual duties of the priests were regularly done, but they were only ritual, always falling short of the reality to which they pointed. God had planned something better, something truly effective in dealing with sin, and that plan would be enacted at "the time for setting things right [by reform]" (9:10). By his death, burial, resurrection and ascension, Jesus entered once for all into the Most Holy Place, taking not the blood of goats and bulls but "his own blood, and has secured an eternal redemption for us" (9:12). God's final plan is to "cleanse our conscience from dead works so that we can rightly serve the living God" (9:14). Jesus carries believers beyond the limitations of ritual and he breaks the limits imposed upon us by sin. For "Christ did not enter into a holy place made by human hands, which was but a copy of the real, but [actually] into heaven itself, and he now appears in the presence of God on our behalf" (9:24). There he will remain, ministering as the eternal High Priest "after the order of Melchizedek," until the designated time when he is to "appear [Gk. *ophthesetai,* will show himself] a second time, not to deal with sin, but for [their] salvation" (9:28).

E. Animal Sacrifices Contrasted With Jesus' Sacrificial Death (10:1–18)

Although the writer has already dwelt at some length on the theme of sacrifice, and the related subtheme of the old covenant with its priestly ministry to deal with human sin, he extends his treatment a great deal further in chapter 10. In reading this section of Hebrews, one will recognize much that overlaps with previous statements in chapters 7–9, sometimes an almost verbal repetition, but this time the writer will make his restatement about sacrifices against a new background, declaring that Jesus, by his death, grants "substance" (Gk. *eikon,* "true form," 10:1; or *huparxis,* "reality," 10:34) for our spiritual life, while the ritualism of the old covenant order restricted every worshiper to only a "shadow" (Gk. *skia*) of the reality worshipers need.

1. ANIMAL SACRIFICES ARE BUT "SHADOW" (10:1–4)

10:1–4. No shadow fully reveals or reflects reality, so no animal sacrifice fully availed to deal adequately with human sin. Thus the constant ritual of offering animals in prescribed sacrifice to God. The pattern had to be repeated because human failure was constant, and the need to atone for committed sins was perennial. Thus the writer's words: "For it is not possible for the blood of bulls and goats to take away sins" (10:4).

2. JESUS' OFFERING OF HIMSELF BRINGS REALITY (10:5–18)

10:5–18 The incarnation and sacrificial death of Jesus corrected the human problem and met the unfulfilled need. With a body prepared for him, Jesus fulfilled the righteous will of God as the perfect sacrifice for sins, so that all who believe "have been [truly] cleaned through the offering of the body of Jesus Christ once for all" (10:10). The use here of *ephapax,* meaning "once for all," shows again (as at 7:27 and 9:12) the emphatic finality of Christ's sacrificial death as man's Savior. It was a single sacrifice, "offered for all time" (Gk. *eis to dienekes,* "in perpetuity"), and so efficacious that by this "one offering [only] he has brought to perfection forever those who are [now] being sanctified" (10:14). Believers now live under new covenant terms and experience the anticipated reality: full remission of sins.

F. Exhortation to Experience Access to God Through Jesus (10:19–31)

10:19–31 With the full dismissal of sins, the believer has grounds for a confident freedom to draw near to God "with a true heart and in the full assurance that faith gives" (10:22) and hope (10:23). The approach to God can be made with "confidence" (Gk. *parrhesia,* "openness, freedom"), the implication being that one now has the right to do so because privilege has been extended by what Jesus has accomplished in our interest. This notion of confident freedom in things pertaining to God has been touched upon earlier by the writer at 3:6 and 4:16; in the one passage that confidence stands related to "our hope," and in the other that confidence is encouraged by the expectation of "mercy and grace" from God when we approach him in prayer. According to 10:19, the grounds for such confident freedom of access to God is "the blood of Jesus."

Given the new freedom of access to God and assurance of acceptance by him, the writer sounds his fourth major warning to believers: He encourages them never to return to a life of sinning (10:26–31). To return to a life of deliberate sinning, he argues, is to spurn the Son of God, profane the blood of the new covenant, and insult the Spirit of grace (10:29).

G. Exhortation to Faith and Perseverance (10:32–39)

10:32–39 Chapter 10 closes with a call for the readers to reflect on how God had helped them through a difficult period they had suffered as believers, and to set themselves in readiness to deal with any further pressures they might have to undergo for their faith. He encouraged the readers to will endurance, to remind themselves of the promises of God, and to commit their trust to God's timely care. The promises of God have always been sure and will remain so, even when we humans fail. The crucial word is sounded: "You really need patient endurance, so that after you have done the will of God, you may receive what has been promised" (10:36). What God promises will result, but it cannot be rushed by our impatience. If put into slogan form, the writer was saying: When you must wait on God, don't lose your faith, use your faith!

III. The Meaning and Necessity of Faith (11:1—12:29)

A. Faith Defined (11:1–3)

11:1–3 At many points in his letter the writer has called attention to the need on the part of his readers for "faith" (4:2; 6:1, 12; 10:22). He is now ready to elaborate on what he means by using the word.

Earlier in this letter, the writer has used the word *faith* with two differing but related accents: first, at 10:22, as an assurance of heart about a truth of which one is aware—a settled state of mind; second, at 10:23, 36, and 38, as a personal response toward God's promises—an action being focused. Now in chapter 11 he provides a working definition that calls attention to an attitude of commitment by which one persists and endures when all things seem contrary: "Now faith is firm confidence regarding what is being expected, the proof of what is not [yet] seen" (11:1). It is important to keep this working definition in mind when reading 11:6, which states that "without faith it is not possible to be pleasing to God." It is with this understanding of faith that the writer deals at length in chapter 11, and he illustrates that attitude of trusting commitment by many examples drawn from the Old Testament narratives.

Life with God demands on our part a certain openness to truth and a personal commitment to experience what that truth presents and makes possible. Since truth is God's agency for dealing with us, the writer describes it as the basis of trust. Faith demands "receiving the knowledge of the truth" (10:26), an expression that was current among first-century believers and reflected their understanding of the relation between knowledge and faith, knowledge and committed trust, and action. Faith, then, is a convictional stance toward life and living, a readiness to face life and deal with its circumstances armed with an attitude of trust and the spirit to endure.

B. Faith Illustrated (11:4–40)

11:4–40 This section of the Hebrews letter reports what such a faith did and does for those who dared to live by God's concerns. Intent to supply a catalog of models for his readers, the writer parades a succession of heroes and heroines of faith. The personal experience of each listed person shows how faith worked in them at some crucial juncture in their life. Each person's story allows us to watch individuals wrestle for meaning in contexts that seemed crushing and unmanageable. All of the listed persons responded to life as pilgrims caught between past and future in a very demanding present, and their trust in God's concern for them gave them perspective, patience, and persistence. All were persons of their time, but stirred by the forward look; they were seekers, pulled upon by what was yet to be, encouraged by what they anticipated. They all sensed that the meaning of their days would be clarified in time, and vindicated by God. True faith is characterized by a forward look and an openness to the pull of the future that God has planned.

The writer lamented that lack of time did not allow him to deal fully with the stories of faith, that he had to leave out of his accounting many additional cases in point (11:32–38). He ended the chapter with a word that the rewards of faith are not always immediate and not always totally complete, God having planned that time at the end of history when total fulfillment will be ours.

C. Faith and Disciplined Living (12:1–11)

12:1–11 Chapter 12 begins with a call to structure a personal history that honors the kind of faith illustrated by those who form the great "cloud of witnesses" that surround present believers. The picture in 12:1–2 is that of a sports amphitheater. The spectators seated in the gallery are the many triumphant victors mentioned in chapter 11, and the call to those now feeling the strain and stress of living for God is to be a winner like the others: "Run with perseverance the course set before us" (12:1). Jesus is cited as the supreme proof of what faith enables one to do, but he is also the supreme person whose work nourishes faith in those who look fully to him. Thus that all-important instruction to keep "looking to Jesus." The believer is backed by Jesus—and beckoned forward by him. Victory against sin happens with his help. Looking to him strengthens one to remain loyal to him. "Consider him…so that you may not become weary and faint in your souls" (12:3).

This instruction was urgent and insistent because of the situation of stress the readers were suffering, but according to 12:4, none of the persons in the group being addressed had as yet "resisted to the point of [shedding] their blood," none of them had been put to death for their faith. Nevertheless, the struggle was acute and demanding, and only a stalwart faith could help them to endure with loyalty. The writer suggested that the struggle be viewed as a means of "discipline" (Gk. *paideia,* "instructive training for development") by which God would help them "share his holiness" (12:10). Thus the quotation from Proverbs 3:11–12. The writer's word is that what is painful can be made purposive, instructive, and positive in its issue.

D. Exhortation to Steadfastness in Faith (12:12–17)

12:12–17 Grace can be experienced, but it can also be forfeited if evil is allowed its way in the heart. The writer reminds the readers that there is an attitude of openness to present opportunity that is required if divine favor is to accomplish its purpose in the believer. He illustrates how one can "fail to obtain the grace of God" by citing the short-sighted and selfish attitude of Esau, "who sold his birthright for a single meal" (12:16).

E. The Privileged Position of the Believer (12:18–29)

12:18–29 The believer holds a privileged position that must not be lost by impatience, immorality, bitter attitudes, or lack of trust in God. Believers need to remember and regard where they stand because of the new covenant and live with full openness and loyalty to what it all means. Given all that belongs to our salvation, and with promise of still more to come, the believer's attitude must be one of conscious thanks and a steady reverence, offering to God acceptable worship, "with reverent devotion and awe" (12:28).

IV. Concluding Remarks (13:1–25)

The writer closes his letter with some pertinent exhortations and a final personal word of greeting to his readers. The exhortations are all very brief, so brief indeed that it might appear the writer was rushing to complete what had by now become lengthy. Some scholars view this section as filled with disconnected injunctions that do not follow from what the writer treated earlier in the letter; some other scholars view it as a later addition made to the letter.

Chapter 13 seems integral to the letter in at least four ways: (1) The injunctions listed in 13:1–17 do have some background in what has been set forth thematically in chapters 1–12. (2) The personal request for prayer (13:18–19) restates the writer's confidence in his readers and he promises to visit with them again as soon as possible. (3) The formal benediction in 13:20–21 is a final means for encouraging his readers. And (4) the additional greetings from mutual friends would also grant some encouragement for them. The information shared about Timothy's release (possibly from prison) would also be a reason for hope and praise by that trouble-weary community of believers.

A. Christian Relationships (13:1–6)

13:1–6 The injunctions about "brotherly affection" and "hospitality" were in the interest of strengthening the community bond that belongs to the church. Their life together must be that of family-love, with no selfish individualism. Those who are in trouble, suffering at the hands of people in power, must not be forsaken but sustained. The word about fidelity in marriage warns against immorality and deeds that undermine a stable family order, while the warning against "love of money" is strategic as a value-word about keeping priorities clearly focused for the life of faith. The promise about the unfailing companionship of the Lord with his people relates to any felt threat of loneliness as sufferers, on the one hand, and lostness as pilgrims, on the other.

B. Christian Duties (13:7–17)

13:7–17 There is an emphatic word about honor due to godly leaders (13:7, 17), whose work is essential for congregational health, continuance, and mission. Jesus Christ remains all he was sent to be and does all that his priestly ministry was planned to accomplish. No teachings must be entertained or regarded which differ from what the godly leaders have shared about Jesus and his role; while believers must be open to learn truths of the faith (5:11–14), they must take care to assess all new teaching by truth already known so as not to be "led away" (Gk. *parapheresthe,* literally, "carried away"). Sharing must continue, especially sharing in the sufferings of Jesus, who was treated as an "outsider" (13:12–13). The acknowledging of his name must not cease, whatever the suffering attached to such witness and loyalty as believers.

C. Personal Expressions (13:18–25)

13:18–25 A request for prayer from his readers (13:18–19) is soon balanced by a prayer on the writer's part for them (13:20–21). Such a prayer wish was a familiar benediction in Christian worship, as other New Testament epistles abundantly show.

Unit Reflections

With his message now shared and its long argument concluded, the writer made a personal appeal that his "word of exhortation" be accepted in the spirit of love out of which it has been sent (13:22). The hope is voiced that Timothy, their mutual friend, recently released from confinement, will be able to come along when the writer makes his anticipated visit with his readers. Meanwhile, his hearty greeting must suffice (13:24), allied by greetings from other believers known and loved by them. In his final statement, a prayer—"May God's favor remain with all of you" (13:25)—the writer assures his readers that God's favor is their common provision and their mutual bond.

PART II:

PREACHING FROM HEBREWS

Chapter 3

The Author's Hermeneutic:

Jesus and the Believer

The Letter to the Hebrews is one of the earliest and most extensive written attempts to connect the ancient Hebrew cultus in the Old Testament with the new covenantal order instituted by the death and resurrection of Jesus Christ. With clear knowledge of the ancient system and an acute sensitivity to its prophetic importance, the writer identified historical personages and dramatic events within Israel's past, intent on providing the theological meaning of covenant and law, sacrifice and worship, and how all these pointed beyond themselves to the redemptive mission of Jesus. The writer's interpretative procedure was blessed by ardent reflection, and the understandings which fed that reflection are quite explicit as one examines his letter.

The Author as an Interpreter

First of all, the writer of Hebrews was inspired by the understanding that God has spoken most fully and finally in Jesus his Son. The foundation of his hermeneutic stands revealed in the opening line of the letter, which states that throughout Israel's history God has been experienced as speaker to his people.

Second, the writer was equipped with an additional and explanatory word about Jesus, a word of illumination that is continuous with what the apostles of Christ preached in spreading the message of "salvation" (2:3). The writer labels their allied testimony a "confession" (*homologia,* 3:1; 4:14; 10:23; 11:13; 13:15). The entire letter is a confession of faith, a confession of beliefs stirred by a rehearsal of historical names and events weighted with soteriological meanings. The life and ministry of Jesus the Son are always in view, and the treatment given him was to put objection, negation, doubt, and apostasy to shame. Every pointed detail is relevant and revealing.

Third, he had equipped himself with strategic scriptures by which to address, anchor, and advance the faith of those being addressed. Several scriptural passages were key resources for him (especially from the Pentateuch, the Psalms, and Jeremiah 31:31–34), and he exposed the doctrinal significance of those texts to expound their implications for the obedience of faith. The writer was a wise preacher. He selectively drew upon the Scriptures, alert to locate and state only what is of primary importance to give his solemn but stately witness. Markus Barth has commented that "the author of Hebrews distinguishes qualitatively among different elements of the Old Testament; only the better things attested are immediate references to Christ."[1]

The writer approached the Old Testament influenced by apostolic preaching, on the one hand, and by a personal faith-interaction with each text, on the other. He dealt with the gospel tradition within known norms, but he was intent on tracing out the background and implications of that

---

1. Markus Barth, *Conversation with the Bible* (New York: Holt, Rinehart and Winston, 1964), p. 219. See also Markus Barth, "The Old Testament in Hebrews," in *Current Issues in New Testament Interpretation: Essays in Honor of Otto A. Piper*, edited by William Klassen and Graydon F. Snyder (New York and Evanston, IL: Harper & Row, 1962) For some additional studies about the writer's appropriation and use of the Old Testament in Hebrews, see also George Howard, "Hebrews and the Old Testament Quotations," *Novum Testamentum*, vol. X (1968), pp. 208–16; J. C. McCullough, "The Old Testament Quotations in Hebrews," *New Testament Studies*, vol. 26, pp. 363–79; Matthew Black, "The Theological Appropriation of the Old Testament by the New Testament," *Scottish Journal of Theology*, vol. 39, no.1 (1986), pp. 1–17; H. Anderson, "The Jewish Antecedents of the Christology in Hebrews," in *The Messiah: Developments in Earliest Judaism and Christianity*, edited by James H. Charlesworth (Minneapolis: Fortress Press, 1992), especially pp. 527–28.

gospel by drawing upon the Scriptures, collective record, and hopes of Israel. Those sacred texts livingly moved within his thought; he felt their impact and sensed their import. He saw established links between the old order of sacrifices and the new message about the sacrificial death of Jesus. So he referred his readers back to the leaders, experiences, longings, promises, Scriptures, and hopes of the Jewish nation in order to move those readers forward in their understanding and faith. For him, the Old Testament texts pointed to the superior event that has taken place in the person of Jesus, and he was eager to restate, interpret, and make that event understandable to help believers have a strengthened faith and a sustained hope.

The writer's vivid interpretation of Jesus as high priest stands out as a unique statement in the New Testament. Floyd V. Filson commented about the writer:

> He shows agreement with the Christian writers of his time, but he is no mere echo or duplicate of any contemporary author. It will be a great gain if we can hear him speak in his own way and let him put the emphasis on his own key issues of Christian faith and thought, and the Church may listen with profit to what he has to say to our later day.[2]

The writer knew the fixed elements of the gospel witness. He knew the facts of the ministry, death, resurrection, and ascension of Jesus. He knew, as George R. Beasley-Murray has stated, that "the acts of God in Christ constituted the gospel."[3] But to him, the "gospel," the "good news," included all of the gracious dealings of God throughout history, with the cross event as the highest expression of that grace.

---

2. Floyd V. Filson, *"Yesterday" A Study of Hebrews in the Light of Chapter 13* ("Studies in Biblical Theology," Second Series 4) (London: SCM Press Ltd., 1967), p. 7.

3. George R. Beasley-Murray, *Preaching the Gospel from the Gospels* (London: Lutterworth Press, 1956), p. 14.

Interestingly, the noun *euaggelion*, "gospel," does not appear at all in Hebrews, but the verb *euaggelizo*, "to preach good news," appears twice. It appears first in 4:2, where the reference is to how the nation wandered for years and missed gaining the "rest" God promised because of disobedience and unbelief:

> For the good news came *[eueggelismenoi*, perfect passive] to us just as to them; but the message they heard did not benefit them, because it did not meet with faith in those who listened.

The verb appears next at 4:6.

> Since therefore it remains for some to enter [rest] and those who formerly received the good news *[euaggelisthentes*, aorist passive] failed to enter because of disobedience ....

Perhaps the writer was influenced by the Septuagint passages where *euaggelizesthai* appears (Isa 40:9; 52:7; 60:6; 61:1). Like Paul, the writer of Hebrews appropriated the term with special consideration for the content of the news being shared, but, unlike Paul, he understood "gospel" in the wider sense described above, with the cross event as the supreme act of divine grace toward humans.

It is in connection with that wider sense of "gospel" that his frequent use of the word *promise [epaggelia]* must be understood and valued. For our writer, the word *promise* must be understood as "good news." He associated every divine promise with some announced good or grand benefit for those willing to receive it on God's terms.[4] He viewed every divine promise as a basis for "hope" *(elpis,* 3:6; 6:11, 18; 7:19; 10:23; 11:1). He honored God as "the promising One" (10:23), who is faithful, aware that hope can

---

4. See 4:1; 6:12, 17; 7:6; 8:6; 9:15; 10:36; 11:13; 17:39. See also the use of *epaggellomai* at 10:23, in particular.

Preaching from Hebrews

be born when God speaks, is nourished as God acts, and is fulfilled when the word of promise has yielded its intended result. The promises of God are always special. In making a promise, God announces an intention, and the content of the promise is to stir faith, promote expectation, and influence the hearer's attitudes and behavior. Those who resist the divine word, however, forfeit its positive benefits for themselves. Thus the writer's urgent plea at 2:1, "Therefore we must pay greater attention to what we have heard, so that we do not drift away from it," and his strong warning at 12:25, "See that you do not refuse the one who is speaking; for if they did not escape when they refused the one who warned them on earth, how much less will we escape if we reject the one who warns from heaven!"

The Letter to the Hebrews is no traditional presentation of the gospel. This letter constitutes a theological interpretation of how the Old Testament points to Jesus, and in highlighting the role of the resurrected Jesus as Savior and High Priest of those who believe and obey him (5:9), the writer has offered the first existential handling of the kerygma. His handling of the gospel tradition is new and illuminating. While we recognize and admire this on his part, it is important, however, to keep in mind what J. Louis Martyn commented about the Fourth Gospel:

> One thing, at least, is shared by all New Testament authors in this regard: none of them merely repeats the tradition. Everyone hears it in his own present and that means in his own way; everyone shapes it, bends it, makes selections from among its riches, even adds to it. Put in other terms, everyone reverences the tradition enough to make it his own.[5]

The writer's way of explaining the relation of Jesus and the believer opens a new understanding of how a vital faith can qualitatively transform

---

5. J. Louis Martyn, *History and Theology in the Fourth Gospel* (New York and Evanston, IL: Harper & Row, 1968), p. xix.

one's experience of life and grant hope for the future. Through its shared meaning about how God has turned lovingly toward humans in Jesus, this letter helps believers gain a strengthening faith and a steadying morale. The writer wanted his readers to be completely committed to faith in Jesus so as to gain all God has promised in and through him. Here, again, the letter's accent on "promise" is seen because, as F. F. Bruce has reminded us, in Hebrews promise is always linked with the corollary fact of fulfillment.[6]

Jesus' Relation to God and Believers

1. Jesus, God's Son

The Letter to the Hebrews begins with a high Christology couched in hymnic lines. Whether verses 1–4 contain lines borrowed from a church hymn or were fashioned by the writer remains a question, but their kerygmatic message regarding Jesus as God's Son is clear and forceful. The designation of Jesus as "Son" *(huios)* in 1:2 immediately defines his relationship to the God he represents and for whom he speaks. Soon afterward, at 2:5–18, the writer speaks about the Son "sharing in flesh and blood" (2:14) to show the relationship between Jesus and humans in general and believers in particular. That Jesus took on humanness and became fully involved in human experience was in order to "bring many children to glory" (2:10) and because believers honor the same God as Father: "For this reason Jesus is not ashamed to call them brothers and sisters" (2:11). His sharing in "flesh and blood" was full. He "became like his brothers and sisters in every respect, so that he might be a merciful and faithful high priest in the service of God, to make a sacrifice of atonement for the sins of the people" (2:17). The message is that Jesus is fully identified with God as Son and with humankind as an experiencing person. Three aspects of the Son's ministry are introduced as the letter begins in 1:1–4: the Son

---

6. F. F. Bruce, "Hebrews," in *Peake's Commentary on the Bible,* edited by Matthew Black and H. H. Rowley (London: Thomas Nelson and Sons, Ltd., 1963), p. 1008.

spoke God's final word during his earthly life; the Son's expiatory work has effected purification of sins; and the Son has been exalted as High Priest.

Jesus is steadily honored throughout Hebrews as the divine Son (1:2, 5, 8; 3:6; 4:14; 5:5, 8; 6:6; 7:28; 10:29), but the emphasis placed on his sonship is never at the expense of the features of his real humanity and earthly experiences. In fact, "the Epistle to the Hebrews itself outdoes all other books, always excepting the gospels and Acts, in safeguarding the real humanity of Jesus."[7] While only a few historical details about Jesus are mentioned in the Pauline writings—that he was born to a Jewish woman (Gal 4:4); that he was a descendant of David (Rom 1:3); that he was betrayed (1 Cor 11:23), was crucified (1 Cor 2:2; Phil 2:8), was buried and raised from death (1 Cor 15:4; Rom 6:4)—Hebrews centers considerable attention upon the earthly life of Jesus in order to highlight his meaning for others. Every historical detail mentioned about Jesus—the substance of his preaching (2:3), his struggle experience in the Gethsemane garden (5:7–8), his physical heritage as a tribal descendant of Judah (7:14), his death on a cross (6:6; 12:2), and his resurrection (13:20)—was made to strengthen faith and fortitude. The writer knew that his argument gained relevance only in connection with a clearly stated set of details about the earthly Jesus.

2. Jesus, God's Final Spokesman

Following mention in 1:1–2 about the work of prophets to the Hebrew nation across its history, the writer declared that God's Son has spoken more fully about his will and ways. A specific tradition about Jesus' preaching is in view in 2:3 when "salvation" [*soteria*] is mentioned as his declared subject matter. This reflection about what Jesus preached links his word with what the apostles began to preach. The writer's statement that what the apostles

---

7. William Kendrick Grobel, "The Human Jesus Outside the Gospels and Acts," in *New Testament Sidelights: Essays in Honor of Alexander Converse Purdy*, edited by Harvey K. McArthur (Hartford, CT: Hartford Seminary Foundation Press, 1960), p. 86.

preached during their ministry "was declared at first through the Lord" demands strict attention because, as Brooke Foss Westcott has explained, it "suggests somewhat more than the simple fact *having first been spoken,* and implies that the teaching of the Lord was the true origin of the Gospel."[8] Something more must be said in this connection, however, because the words of the Son supersede the word spoken by prophets and angels; all the prophets and angels spoke as functioning servants, but the Son spoke with greater authority and with finality because of his character and relationship to God (1:2).

Throughout Hebrews, the theme of speech and hearing appears, with prophets (1:1), angels (2:2), the Son (1:2; 2:3), the Holy Spirit (3:7,15) and even God himself mentioned as addressing humans (11:8; 12:19, 25–27; 13:5b). As the final speaker for God, Jesus as God's Son fulfills a unique function and holds an incomparable dignity. Prophets came and spoke "bit by bit," and with diverse giftedness, their words successive and supplementary, pointing always beyond themselves to God. In his coming, the Son has spoken with fullness and finality, in "these last days," revealing God's character (1:3) as well as voicing God's gracious but final call. His word announced, promised, and dispenses "salvation" (2:3; 5:9).[9]

---

8. Brooke Foss Westcott, *The Epistle to the Hebrews: The Greek Text with Notes and Essays* (Grand Rapids, MI: Wm. B. Eerdmans Publishing Co., 1892), p. 39.

9. In connection with the statement in 5:9, that Jesus "became the source of eternal salvation for all who obey him," that obedience presupposes a "hearing" of the word about salvation, and "obeying" that word requires some instructions to be followed. Thus the call of Jesus for hearers to "repent" (Matt 4:17; Luke 13:3, 5; 24:47). The apostles addressed hearers with the same call (Mark 6:12; Acts 2:38; 3:19; 17:30; 20:21; 26:20). According to Paul, the standard instruction for the hearer to receive salvation is for his or her "repentance toward God and faith towards our Lord Jesus" (Acts 20:21) and to "confess with [the] lips that Jesus is Lord…raised from the dead" (Rom 10:9). The writer of Hebrews keeps the same imperatives in view in his letter in his frequent reference to "our confession" (*homologia,* 3:1; 4:14; 10:23; 13:15).

3. Jesus, the All-Sufficient Sacrifice for Sins

Emphasizing the real humanity of the Son was foundational for the message about his self-offering as an atoning sacrifice to God. Jesus was readied for this aspect of his mission by (a) receiving a body (2:14; 10:5b, 10), which made him death-eligible, and (b) by successfully passing all tests as a human to become "perfected" for his role as a sacrifice (4:15; 5:8–9). That word *perfected (teleioo)* is a term of breadth and fullness; it means "up to standard, fully adequate," readied, fit. The use of the term here was probably with cultic overtones, meaning to be consecrated or readied for presentation to God as a sacrifice.[10] The end result, the writer states, was that "he became the source of eternal salvation for all who obey him" (5:9).

Hebrews 5:7–10 holds some illuminating insights regarding God's appointment of Jesus to that sacrificial role. In 5:5 the writer appears to have used Psalm 2:7 to add another element to the tradition about the baptism of Jesus by John. Knowing that Jesus entered upon his ministry with a strong sense of vocation and destiny, the writer viewed that Psalm-text as God's words of appointment both to Jesus' sacrificial service and to his high priestly role, and at 9:14 he viewed the descent of the Spirit upon Jesus after being baptized as preparation for his eventual death as a sacrifice for sins. Vincent Taylor commented, "It's reasonable to infer that His sense of a suffering destiny is lineally connected with the initial experience of baptism."[11] This treatment in

---

10. On the lexical meaning, see Walter Bauer, *A Greek-English Lexicon of the New Testament and Other Early Christian Literature*, trans. by William F. Arndt and F. Wilbur Gingrich, 2nd ed. rev. by F. Wilbur Gingrich (Chicago: University of Chicago Press, 1979), pp. 809–10. On its theological usage in the verse, see R. Schippers, "*teleioo*," in *The New International Dictionary of New Testament Theology*, edited by Colin Brown, vol. 2 (Grand Rapids, MI: Zondervan Publishing House, 1976), pp. 63–64; Hans Hubner, s.v., in *Exegetical Dictionary of the New Testament*, vol. 3, edited by Horst Balz and Gerhard Schneider (Grand Rapids, MI: Wm. B. Eerdmans Publishing Co., 1993), p.345.

11. Vincent Taylor, *The Gospel According to St. Mark: The Greek Text, with Introduction, Notes and Indexes* (London: Macmillan Co., Ltd., 1963), p. 619. See also Thomas W. Manson, *The Servant-Messiah: A Study of the Public Ministry of Jesus* (Cambridge, England:

Hebrews of the baptism of Jesus underscores the fact that Jesus acted always in God's will, humbly obeying God, stirred and sustained by the desire to "fulfill all righteousness," as Jesus said to John while being baptized (Matt 3:14–15). Perhaps that same tradition about what Jesus said to John the Baptizer also influenced the writer to use Psalm 45:7 at Hebrews 1:9:

> You have loved righteousness and hated wickedness; therefore God, your God, has anointed you with the oil of gladness beyond your companions.

At any rate, the obedience of Jesus to God is in view at Hebrews 5:5–10, and that obedience was demonstrated supremely when Jesus humbled himself to die "to remove sin by the sacrifice of himself" (9:26)

Hebrews 5:7 recalls details of the passion Jesus experienced as he prayed in the Garden of Gethsemane:

> In the days of his flesh, Jesus offered up prayers and supplications, with loud cries and tears, to the one who was able to save him from death, and he was heard because of his reverent submission.

The writer does not expressly state that this was the same experience about which the Gospel writers have reported (Matt 26:36–46; Mark 14:32–42; Luke 22:39–46; John 12:27), nor does he quote any of the words of Jesus those writers preserved, but this part of the Passion story was in circulation within the church, and the writer clearly saw how its use could both enlighten and encourage.

The humanity of Jesus is in clear view in Hebrews 5:7, and his reaction to a real situation of threat is described with vividness. The account reports something about the way God helped Jesus to handle himself, but

---

Cambridge University Press, 1953), especially pp. 45–46, 65; George R. Beasley-Murray, *Baptism in the New Testament* (London: Macmillan and Co. Ltd., 1963), especially pp. 45–67.

something is also being suggested in the account for the believer to understand about the need to cultivate a "reverent submission" to the will of God. The scene in the account keeps one aware that Jesus was a deciding subject before he was declared a Savior. Using his freedom responsibly, Jesus prayed, offering up "prayers and supplications, with loud cries and tears, to the one who was able to save him from death." Jesus made his request with freedom, with earnestness, with human assertiveness, and in pain. But he prayed to God as God, responding to God's presence and to the nature of his plight in the spirit of a "reverent submission" (*eulabeia*), which involves something more than self-interest. The result after the prayer was that God moved Jesus beyond the facts of his situation: "he was heard because of his reverent submission."

What was the situation that prodded Jesus to offer to God such "prayers and supplications, with loud cries and tears"? He asked God to save him from "death" *(thanatos)*. Many questions rise and clamor to be answered as one reads verse 7. Did Jesus offer those prayers and make those supplications because he was humanly frustrated? Was he, being human, only experiencing existential dread, the discontent and dis-ease that comes when facing one's mortality? Was his prayer-protest to live generated, as in most humans, by a preoccupation with life? Or was Jesus dealing with something more than natural feelings? Could he have prayed that way to avert dying in the garden?

To be sure, the record states that Jesus prayed to be saved from death, yet we know that he came "to remove sin by the sacrifice of himself" (9:26; 10:10). The writer's line of argument in Hebrews 2:9–10, 14–15 helps greatly to place the apparent problem in 5:7 in perspective. The writer explains fear of death as a power wielded by the Devil, who uses the fear of dying to hold persons "in slavery" (2:15b), wearying them with anxiety and dread. *Death* is a recurring word in Hebrews: It is an experience humans suffer, a happening that provokes an enslaving fear that the Devil uses to threaten and inflict pain (2:14–15).

Jesus came to "taste death for everyone" (2:9), to deal with death on behalf of, in the interest of, everyone. According to Hebrews 5:7, Jesus was "heard," presumably meaning more than the fact that God listened to the prayer, rather that God answered his request to be saved from death. The Greek construction behind "from death" is instructive: *ek thanatou* can be viewed to mean Jesus was saved from dying while praying under pressure in the Garden—from agonies which Luke 22:43–44 described, including bloody sweat falling from his body as he prayed; or it can be viewed to mean that Jesus was resurrected *out of* death after his voluntary death on the cross.[12]

4. Jesus, the Exalted High Priest

All the realities of redemption and a godly life connect in and issue from Jesus, who has triumphed over death. He is alive (7:24–25), he has ascended (8:1; 10:12), he is accessible (4:15–16), and he assures each believer mercy and grace to approach God as his children—brothers and sisters of Jesus—in the household of faith

---

12. On the view that Jesus was spared from dying in the Garden, see Thomas Hewitt, *The Epistle to the Hebrews: Introduction and Commentary* (Grand Rapids, MI: Wm. B. Eerdmans Publishing Co., 1960), especially pp. 99–101. On the Lukan passage (22:43–44) about the bloody sweating Jesus suffered as he prayed, some manuscripts include it while some others do not. I. Howard Marshall, among others, views that passage as based on "some floating tradition which had not found its way into the Synoptic tradition." See I. Howard Marshall, *The Gospel of Luke: A Commentary on the Greek Text* (New International Greek Testament Commentary) (Grand Rapids, MI: Wm. B. Eerdmans Publishing Co., 1978), p. 831. For a contrary view, see John Nolland, *Luke 18:35–24:53* (Word Biblical Commentary, 35c) (Dallas: Word Books, 1993), p. 1084. On some of the problems exegetes face in dealing with the difficult closing phrase of Hebrews 5:7, "he was heard," see, among others, Neil R. Lightfoot, "The Saving of the Savior: Hebrews 5:7ff," *Restoration Quarterly*, vol. 16, nos. 3,4, Third and Fourth Quarter 1973, pp. 166–73.

(3:6; 416; 12:7).[13] Influenced by Old Testament terminology, on the one hand, and by the house church arrangement, on the other, the writer used the primary social structure in those days to underscore the social structure of the church. Being members of the "house-hold" (= church), believers have privileges and duties. As for privileges, believers are under God's care and have access to the Father (4:16; 12:23); as for duties, there is the imperative to obey God's voice (3:6–15; 12:25), and there is an obligation to seek the welfare of other believers (13:1–3, 7, 16, 18). Hebrews offers very little regarding church order, and that little appears in connection with the "household" image, with Jesus "over God's house as a Son" (3:6) and as High Priest (10:21). James D. G. Dunn has rightly remarked, "The most striking feature of Hebrews at this point however is the way the *ministry focuses in Christ in a complete and final manner.*"[14]

In discussing the priestly ministry of Jesus "in the heavens," the writer built upon a fundamental article of early Christian faith. Oscar Cullmann has explained that "the centre of the high priestly work is Jesus' earthly act of sacrifice, but the present office of mediation emphasizes the work of the risen Lord, the aspect which actually interested the Church above all."[15]

---

13. The writer of the Letter to the Hebrews was influenced by the Old Testament's people of God motif, so he views the church as a family or "household." The household image is reflected in the passages about believers as "brothers" [*adelphoi*], believers as "children" [*paidia*], and believers as "sons" [*huioi*]. Recent translations seek to be gender inclusive by adding "and daughters" where "sons" appear in the text or, as in 12:7, by substituting "children" for "brothers" or "sons."

14. James D. G. Dunn, *Unity and Diversity in the New Testament: An Inquiry into the Character of Earliest Christianity* (Philadelphia: Westminster Press, 1977), p. 119. The italics are by Dunn. See also Eduard Schweizer, *Church Order in the New Testament* (London: SCM Press, 1961), section 10c. See also Paul S. Minear, *Images of the Church in the New Testament* (Philadelphia: Westminster Press, 1960), pp. 165–72.

15. Oscar Cullmann, *The Christology of the New Testament* (Philadelphia: Westminster Press, 1963, rev. ed), p. 104. Trans. by Shirley Guthrie and Charles A. M. Hall.

Drawing upon texts from a known collection used liturgically and in the cultic framework of Israel's worship settings, the writer of Hebrews developed his argument about the high priestly work of Jesus within a familiar hermeneutical context. Psalm 110 was of cardinal importance in attesting his "witness" concerning this aspect of the ministry of Jesus. Barnabas Lindars has commented, "It is not too much to say that the entire Christology of this Epistle stems from the study of this psalm." And further, "It is universally recognized that the Christological application of Psalm 110:1 is of cardinal importance throughout the New Testament."[16] That Psalm 110:1ff was interpreted messianically at an early time in the church is clearly evident from the many citations given its verses in the Gospels and Epistles.[17] The Gospel tradition reports that Jesus used Psalm 110 on two specific occasions and interpreted the lines he quoted as applying to himself (Matt 22:41–46; 26:62–64).

Given the importance of Jesus as incarnate Son, the all-sufficient sacrifice, and exalted High Priest, it is all the more important for believers to keep "looking to Jesus the pioneer and perfecter of our faith" (12:2). Such looking keeps one mindful of the example Jesus set in his living and open to the hope his life inspires. Keeping Jesus in view keeps one consciously linked with Jesus as a sharer in his life, a recipient of his mediating work, and a steadfast follower in faith.

Hebrews has more to say about Jesus: Jesus is the believer's *prodromos,* "forerunner" (6:20), who has gone ahead in the interest of those who follow behind. He is also the *archegos,* "pioneer" (2:10), to whose path we follow. These terms as applied to Jesus should remind us, as Eduard Schweizer states, that his work "has a basic character and does not only illustrate

---

16. Barnabas Lindars, *New Testament Apologetic: The Doctrinal Significance of Old Testament Quotations* (Philadelphia: Westminster Press, 1961), p. 51.

17. See, among others, David M. Hay, *Glory at the Right Hand: Psalm 110 in Early Christianity* (Nashville, TN: Abingdon Press, 1973).

discipleship but is the only thing that makes discipleship possible."[18] Since Jesus is *prodromos,* the goal for the believer has been divinely determined. And because Jesus is also *poimen,* "shepherd" (13:20), the believer's need for guidance, companionship, and solidarity is supremely met.

Given these understandings about the significance of Jesus, the writer warned his readers not to forfeit the gains granted them through the new covenant Jesus established through his death (9:15). The readers were encouraged to renew their faith in Jesus. They were warned not to become negligent (2:1), bitter (12:15), immoral (12:16), or ensnared by the love of money (13:5), but the most severe warning was against "falling away" *(parapesontas,* 6:6), changing their mind about Jesus. The penalty for doing so is stated at 10:26, where the explanation is given that "if we willfully persist in sin after having received the knowledge of the truth, there no longer remains a sacrifice for sins," since one has thereby "spumed the Son of God, profaned the blood of the covenant…and outraged [*enubrisas,* insulted, affronted] the Spirit of grace" (10:29). The previous warning at 6:6 also suggests that an anti-Jesus enmity is in the writer's view, an attitude of contempt, mockery, ridicule for the message about, and the person of, Jesus. The wording at 6:4–6 is rigorous and clear:

> For it is impossible to restore again to repentance those who have once been enlightened, and have tasted the heavenly gift, and have shared in the Holy Spirit, and have tasted the goodness of the word of God and the powers of the age to come, and then have fallen away, since on their own they are crucifying again the Son of God and are holding him up to contempt.

---

18. Eduard Schweizer, *Lordship and Discipleship* (Studies III Biblical Theology, No. 28) (London: SCM Press, Ltd., 1960), p. 90.

The problem described is the radical reversal of faith in Jesus, a decisive renunciation of him. The person who does so is classified in 10:27 as an insolent adversary worthy of divine judgment.

The warning concerns a forfeited salvation, through apostasy.[19] Such rebellious turning from the faith was not a hypothetical case but a genuine one for Christians during times of persecution at the hands of civil authorities. That some who belonged to the church turned against it out of interest to escape persecution has been well documented, and their rejection was viewed by many as a final sin. *The Shepherd of Hermas,* a second-century work by Hermas of Rome (c. AD 100–140), deals with how grace could be renewed and one's guilt for having renounced faith could be remitted. As the Catholic tradition was emerging (AD 100–400), before Christianity became the established religion of the empire world, church authorities had to consider not only how apostates are to be regarded but also how due penance or "satisfaction to the Lord" for post-baptismal sins could be made?[20] During the periods when Christians were viewed by the Roman system as anti-Roman, as overthrowers of the ancient religions, and upsetters of the prevailing social order, ardent Christians gave their witness about Jesus as Lord at great cost.[21] Despite all adversities suffered,

19. See Dale Moody, *Apostasy: A Study in the Epistle to the Hebrews and in Baptist History* (Greenville, SC: Smyth & Helwys Publishing, Inc., 1991).

20. See Jaroslav Pelikan, *The Christian Tradition: A History of the Development of Doctrine,* vol. I (Chicago: University of Chicago Press, 1971), especially pp. 147, 158, 309; J. N. D. Kelly, *Early Christian Doctrines* (London: Adam & Charles Black, 1960 sec. ed.), especially pp. 216–19; Leonhard Goppelt, *Apostolic and Post-Apostolic Times* (London: Adam & Charles Black, 1970), especially pp. 169–74; R. S. T. Haselhurst, *Some Accounts of Penitential Discipline of the Early Church in the First Four Centuries* (London: S.P.C.K., 1921); Oscar D. Watkins, *A History of Penance,* vols. 1 and 2 (London: Longmans, Green, & Co., 1920).

21. Among the many studies, see W. M. Ramsay, *The Church in the Roman Empire: Before A.D. 170* (New York: G. P. Putnam's Sons, 1893), especially pp. 171–374; Francis X. Murphy, *Politics and the Early Christian* (New York and Rome: Desclee Co., 1967), especially pp. 68–88; E. Glenn Hinson, *The Evangelization of the Roman Empire* (Macon, GA: Mercer University Press, 1981), especially pp. 111–29, 233–45. For studies on how the Romans viewed Christians, see Stephen Benko, *Pagan Rome and the Early Christians* (Bloomington,

however, loyalty to Jesus and covenantal concern for the community were expected on the part of every believer. No laxity was to be tolerated. The statements of Jesus about openly acknowledging him before others (Matt 10:32–33; Luke 12:8–9) were not viewed as negotiables. Personally confessing the *homologia* (3:1; 4:14; 10:23) required faithfulness to Jesus and solidarity with other believers, and those who violated the terms of partnership in the faith were stringently censored, not only by the writer of Hebrews, but also by Paul (1 Cor 5:1–5; 1 Tim 1:20; 5:20; 2 Thess 3:6), John (1 John 5:16–17), and Jude (vv 3–4, 22–23).

IN: Indiana University Press, 1984); Robert L. Wilken, *The Christians as the Romans Saw Them* (New Haven, CT: Yale University Press, 1984).

The Author's Hermeneutic   *91*

Chapter 4

Themes of "Holiness" and "Perfection"

Hebrews 12:7–11 encourages believers to consider the trials of life as means by which God trains us for a fuller life in his will, and indeed to view trials as agencies to shape us increasingly in likeness to God. The writer uses as analogy the way a concerned earthly parent seeks to mold a child's character through applying needed discipline. The final thrust of the comparison is found in verse 10, and the teaching of the passage is razor-sharp in its theological implications: "For they disciplined us for a short time as seemed best to them, but he disciplines us for our good, in order that we may share his holiness." The particularity of that wording shows us the writer's theology regarding the spiritual life of the Christian believer.

The wording in verse 12:10, together with the writer's insistence in 12:14 to "pursue holiness," draws attention to one of the most pertinent and positive claims found in the New Testament regarding Christian experience, namely this: God has ordained that those who surrender to his love and obediently follow his Son will increasingly share in likeness to God. There is a much wider catena of texts in Hebrews that deal with the same conspicuous claim. These texts inform us for a needed consideration of the results upon character produced by faith in Jesus and an experience of God, "the Holy One."

Just what is involved in the experience of sharing God's holiness? How does one gain such an experience? What is the believer's posture or position because of that experience? What are the inward and personal aspects of sharing that holiness? What are the outward, social effects? The writer has answered these questions in this epistle.

God as "The Holy One"

Every serious student of Scripture knows that the central concept in its vast teaching about God is God's holiness. This descriptive word about the nature of God occurs with such frequency and emphasis that it cannot be missed or overlooked. Holiness is the basic and key concept for understanding the witness of both testaments concerning God, both as to God's nature and to God's relations with humans, places, and objects. As regards the divine nature, God is referred to, and speaks self-referentially, as "the Holy One" (Job 6:10; Isa 10:17). Another description relates God to the chosen people as "the holy One of Israel" (2 Kings 19:22; Ps 71:22; Isa 1:4b; Jer 51:5; Ezek 39:7).

As "the Holy One," God is distinctly other, separated, marked off in nature from that which is ordinary, human, common, earthly. The otherness of God is so distinctive and unique, so absolute in its perfection and purity, so utterly peculiar to deity, that it occasions a radical awe in humans when God deigns by some mode to confront us. Both Testaments supply us with multiplied instances when humans recoiled upon confronting the *mysterium tremendum*, as Rudolf Otto aptly termed it.[1]

But God is the holy Person. This means that God's otherness does more than stir a radical awe in those confronted by the divine presence; God's otherness also occasions a radical attractiveness that invites. The God of Abraham, Isaac, and Jacob, the God of the Testaments, the God and Father of Jesus the Christ is uniquely separate in nature but neither remote nor utterly removed as a relating Person. God relates to creation

---

1. See Rudolf Otto, *The Idea of the Holy.* (London: Oxford University Press, 1923), pp. 12–24. Trans. by J. W. Harvey.

and with humans. The clearest pictures in Scripture of divine action show concern on God's part to relate with humans and share increasingly with us. This is the dominating theme of the Scriptures.

Since this is so, it is important to ask in what way, and to what extent, does God share the divine holiness with us? It is over this precise question that the theological camps stand divided, some advocates claiming more than God has made available and others claiming less than God intended to bestow. There is a proper claim, because Scripture speaks so readily about this whole matter, and the verses found at 12:10 and 12:14 in Hebrews are chief among the many texts that concern Christian holiness. All Christendom commonly understands and affirms that God relates intimately with believers, but some advocates of this common affirmation assert that God's holiness is only imputed to believers, while some others assert that holiness is actually imparted to us. The holiness-texts in Hebrews encourage us to experience God with such openness that God's holiness becomes a shared benefit in our lives.

As part of his witness, the writer of Hebrews affirmed that God has shown us the divine holiness on our human level in Jesus the Son, whom he described as "holy, blameless, undefiled, separated from sinners" (7:26). As we have seen, the writer of Hebrews sought to stress the meaning of the Sonship of Jesus as a real and revelational sonship. The character of Jesus' life was a manifestation of holiness, i.e., the likeness of God, in the flesh. The writer had earlier stated that Jesus the Son "is the reflection of God's glory and the exact imprint of God's very being" (1:3). The witness of the New Testament is unanimous in declaring that Jesus expresses the divine mode of being on our human level. In Jesus, divine holiness has shown itself in *sarx*, and although he is fully human, that holiness is undiminished. The New Testament writers who gave witness to his life did not get sidetracked over metaphysical questions regarding his genesis or descent as divine Son; they rightly and wisely celebrated Jesus as the holy

Son and saving Person, giving honor to God the Father. What they saw in Jesus began to evidence itself in them through being in his company and walking in his Spirit.

It has been necessary to make this statement about Jesus as the holy Son because what believers are to share of the holiness of God is related to what we see in Jesus. We see his Sonship and. upon accepting him, are granted sonship in his name. As John 1:12 puts it, "But to all who received him, who believed on his name, he gave power to become children of God." Like John, the writer of Hebrews also refers to believers as "children" (2:14; 12:5,7, 8) of God, but prefers to address them as "brothers [and sisters]" (2:11; 3:1, 12; 10:19; 13:22). His approach reflects an ecclesiology that is influenced by the Old Testament people of God motif, with believers forming a family or "household" (see 3:6; 10:21; 12:18–24). This usage was quite widely honored within the Christian community of the first century, a result influenced by Old Testament terminology, on the one hand, and perhaps by the house church arrangement, on the other. But the description of the believing community as a "household" is more than a concept, it argues a social structure under God. God determines and administers the believing community, whose members have privileges and duties, the chief privileges being full family membership (2:10–11) and full access to God as Father (4:16; 12:22–24). Unlike Paul and John, who both showed a fondness for using *teknon*, "child," and its diminuitive *teknion*, "little child," when referring to believers in their relation to God, the writer of Hebrews favored the term *huios*, "son."[2] He honored Jesus as God's exalted Son (1:2; 3:6; 4:14; 5:8; 6:6; 7:3, 28; 10:29), but he also stressed

---

2. Interestingly, John not only used the terms *teknon* ("child") and *teknion* ("little child") for the believer's relation to God, but he also restricted his use of the term *huios* ("son") to Jesus. On this, see Raymond E. Brown, *The Epistles of John* (The Anchor Bible, vol. 30) (Garden City, NY: Doubleday and Co., Inc., 1982), pp. 213–14, 297–99, 388–89, 655, 707. See also R. Alan Culpepper, "The Pivot of John's Prologue," in *New Testament Studies*, vol. 27 (1980–81), especially pp. 17–19, 24–31.

that believers, followers of Jesus, are "sons [and daughters]" (2:10; 12:5,7), and even "brothers [and sisters]" of Jesus (2:11, 12, 17). This writer does not describe Jesus as the one who gives sonship (as does John 1:12), but points to Jesus as the one who leads the "many children to glory" (2:10). The solidarity of Jesus and other children of God is underscored in 2:11, where the writer emphatically states that they "all have one Father." He then added, "For this reason Jesus is not ashamed to call them brothers and sisters." The teaching given there honors the God-believers relationship, and one of the implications of that relationship has to do with the believer's likeness to God's character, by sharing God's holiness.

Christian "Holiness" and "Perfection"

As in our use of language, there were many determinants at work in the writer's use of his. He was guided in the treatment of his theme by basic Christian beliefs, portions from the treasured heritage from Israel's past, the church culture of his time, questions raised by the faith, and his own experiences as a believer. All of these factors influenced what he wrote, and they conditioned what he meant. The meaning and significance of his use of *holiness* and *perfection*, therefore, need to be clearly understood.

The writer's treatment concerning the believer's holiness can be traced in his (1) statements about holiness and in his (2) prescriptives commending the experience. It is in order now to treat these two designations in more detail because this is crucial to the purpose of our topic.

Semanticists have pointed out that in uttering a sentence in our everyday use of language we do one or more of four things: We make a statement, that is, we assert or affirm some fact. We make an expression, an utterance in which emotion and impulse play a considerable role. We speak a prescriptive, directing that something should be done. We utter performatives, saying something that creates a new state of affairs, like making a promise. We intend any one and all of these ways of speaking to convey meaning. Performatives, however, are of a more critical nature since they have to do with our speech-action in which meaning, emotion, and effect all go along hand-in-hand.[3]

These categories of sentence-function provide us with an interesting measure for discerning the function level of the holiness-texts in Hebrews. "Holiness-texts" are sentence units that utilize one or more of the words based upon the Greek root *HAG-* and, in addition, occur in a context significantly related to the concern for holiness. The study of sentences by function-level and intention has an ancient history. Aristotle categorized sentences in this way long, long ago in his *Poetics,* although he outlined five categories rather than the four descriptive categories mentioned above from the perspective of current semantics.[4] With such tools we have for examining the function level of a biblical text, we can expect to discern more from our study of Scripture and its intended uses.

With respect to holiness-texts in Hebrews, the two categories of statement and prescriptive best clarify the sentence-functions of the writer in the quest to discover the meaning and import he intended.

Beginning with the writer's six uses of *hagiazo* (to consecrate, sanctify, make holy), four are in the statement category: Hebrews 2:11; 9:13; 10:14; and 13:12 all assert or affirm something about holiness in relation to believers. Hebrews 2:11 speaks about "those who are sanctified." Hebrews 9:13 credits the blood of Christ with power to sanctify (or consecrate)

---

3. On these categorical descriptions, see Anders Jeffner, *The Study of Religious Language* (London: SCM Press Ltd., 1972), especially pp. 11–12, 68–104. See also J. L. Austin, *How to Do Things with Words*, ed. by J. O. Urmson (New York: Oxford University Press, 1965); and John Wilson, *Language and the Pursuit of Truth* (Cambridge, England: Cambridge University Press, 1960), especially pp. 47–74.

4. See Aristotle, *The Poetics*, xix.7, trans. by W. Hamilton Fyfe (Loeb Classical Library) (Cambridge, MA: Harvard University Press, 1960), pp. 72–73. See also I. Bywater, *Aristotle on the Art of Poetry* (Oxford, England: Clarendon Press, 1909), p. 258–29; E. J. Revell, "Aristotle and the Accents: The Categories of Speech in Jewish and Other Authors," *Journal of Semitic Studies*, vol. XIX, no.1 (Spring 1974), pp. 19–35.

the human conscience. Hebrews 10:14 states, "For by a single offering he [Jesus] has perfected for all time those who are sanctified." Hebrews 13:12 states that "in order to sanctify [consecrate] the people by his own blood," Jesus suffered and died outside the city gate. Hebrews 10:10 states:

> And it is by God's will that we have been sanctified through the offering of the body of Jesus Christ once for all.

Those five sentences about "making holy" or the sanctifying of believers all serve a statement function, but Hebrews 10:29, the sixth holiness text in which the writer used the verb form *hagiazo*, is of a mixed character that blends statement and expression. Observe this result in the way the writer let emotive pastoral concern and spiritual indignation influence that text:

> How much worse punishment do you think will be deserved by those who have spurned the Son of God, profaned the blood of the covenant by which they were sanctified, and outraged the Spirit of grace?

There is but one appearance in Hebrews of *hagiazmos*, the noun form, which means "holiness" or "consecration" (or sanctification) as an experienced state of being that results in godly actions, and its singular use at 12:14 is clearly in a prescriptive sentence; the verse urges the believer to "pursue peace with everyone, and the holiness without which no one will see the Lord." The prescriptive in Hebrews 12:14, together with the statement-verse in 12:10, the discussion about which began this chapter, clearly makes an assertion and sponsors a claim that helps the believer to organize his or her views about life in the will of God. These two verses call upon the believer to exemplify the character of God as Jesus did. The prescriptive word of the writer to "pursue holiness" is unsparing in stress and demand. The imperative is used with high warrant, strict realism, and decisive intent. The statement-text in 12:10 about God's intent to make the believer share in the divine holiness is clearly doctrinal, and the prescriptive-text in 12:14 for the believer to pursue that holiness is expressively convictional. In reading these holiness-texts from this perspective, we gain a new feel for the life that is possible and expected for the Christian believer. The writer's prescriptive challenges every old and divergent pattern, and illuminates the believer's new possibilities as a "child" of God. His imperative to pursue holiness is more than a demand; it announces an opening into a more intimate and instrumental experience as a believer. The New Testament elsewhere associates the believer's holiness with being a recipient of God's Spirit (as in 1 Cor 3:16–17; 6:9–11, 19–20; 1 Thess 4:3, 7–8); the writer of Hebrews associates the believer's holiness with a sustained obedience to Jesus as "the source of eternal salvation" (5:9) and a disciplined acceptance of the terms of life in the will of God (12:10).

The believer's holiness, then, is a derived holiness made possible through the saving work of Jesus. It is a definite and distinctive life that honors the character of God. One might even say that it is holiness as *imitatio de Christi* since his person, life, teachings, actions, and spirit form the visible norm for Christian conduct and concerns. Just as Jesus imitated God, doing as Son the deeds of Father (John 5:19–20; 8:38–47), the believer imitates Jesus, following him, obeying him (5:9), and living for his interests.

Holiness for the believer is that moral and ethical readiness for life that results from committing our will to God's way as seen in Jesus Christ. Christian holiness involves the human will even as God's own original holiness necessarily involves God's every act of will. Walther Eichrodt rightly stated that God is known in terms of "holy personal will."[5] Obedient discipleship is known and exemplified in terms of personal will anchored in the experience of and commitment to holiness. Again Eichrodt, "In any picture

---

5. See Walther Eichrodt, *Theology of the Old Testament*, Vol. One (Philadelphia: The Westminster Press, 1961), p. 278. Trans. by J. A. Baker.

of the divine nature the moral will must be in the foreground dominating the whole."[6] Christian holiness always involves the will. The experience of being made holy, i.e., being consecrated by God, is procured to the believer by the sacrificial death of Jesus, but that holiness develops and deepens in keeping with the believer's dedication and disciplined openness toward God. What we have before us in this derived holiness is a qualitative life, a life that is both a consequence and a commitment.

1. The believer's share in holiness is, first of all, *individual*. It is personal. The whole self is called into the transaction with God. The will is addressed and engaged. Holiness (or sanctification) must deal with the will because it is in the act of willing that personal life is realized. The will and its actions are the basic ingredients of history, since history has to do with human action and the intentional process, in the main.[7] The peculiar uniqueness of willing is that it proclaims individuality and intentionality. Just as sin involves an intentional, willful act that contradicts divine will, holiness must involve intentional, willful obedience to the divine will. The believer is a self who is always positioned between possibility and actuality, positioned there with some frame of reference by which to understand and relate to one or the other. We are not made holy innocently, but voluntarily in response to God's claim upon us. This is always personal, individual, decisive.

2. The believer's share in holiness is also *identifiable*. New character traits are shaped and deepened under the influencing experience of holiness. Meister Eckhart referred to this result as "a habitual will," by which he

---

6. Ibid., p. 279.

7. On this, see John Macmurray, *The Self as Agent* (London: Faber and Faber, 1957), p. 205, who commented: "What merely happens lies outside the historian's province. He is concerned with natural events and organic processes only in so far as they enter into the activities of human beings and play their part in setting the field for human decisions." See also H. Wheeler Robinson, *The Christian Experience of the Holy Spirit* (New York: Harper and Brothers, 1928), especially pp. 101–2.

meant the will transformed into instinct, bringing about a oneness of self and self-interest. Irenaeus also pointed to this result when he said that the Holy Spirit "adjusts us to God."[8] Experiential holiness is identifiable, principally in the character, behavior, and work of the believer. Paul was treating this as he listed the "fruit of the Spirit" (Gal 5:22–23).

3. The believer's share in holiness is *intelligible*. It makes sense! It is always good sense to live by a behavior pattern that honors God, to live by a principle of selectivity that keeps one obedient to God the Father, as did Jesus, who "loved righteousness and hated wickedness" (Heb 1:9). Holiness has always meant certain limitations, but they are all limitations in the interest of life at its best, the consecration and conservation of every personal power and potential in order to realize the manifest destiny of a true child of God.

4. The believer's share in holiness is also *instrumental*. The experience of holiness is not only processive but productive; it prepares the believer for the service of God. John Wesley knew this, and he spent his mature years teaching about it. Here is one of Wesley's most oft-quoted statements about the instrumental aspects of experiential holiness:

> The Gospel of Christ knows of no religion, but social; no holiness, but social holiness. "Faith working by love" is the length and breadth and depth and height of Christian perfection.[9]

Little wonder, then, that Wesley attacked slavery, the plight of the poor, inhumane prison conditions, social and economic imbalances, and exercised his caring heart against other evils with direct, piquant, and vehe-

---

8. Quoted by F. W. Dillistoue, *The Holy Spirit in the Life of Today* (London: The Canterbury Press, 1946), p. 10.

9. *The Works of the Rev. John Wesley*, A.M., (London: John Mason, 1856), vol. 14, p. 305.

ment indignation.[10] The experience of holiness deals with more than the individual development and discipline of the self in the will of God. It is a decisively instrumental experience that readies the believer for social engagement as God's servant, daring to take on necessary tasks in the world.

The teaching in Hebrews about the believer's "holiness" stands related to its teaching about the believer's "perfection." The concern for *teliosis*, "perfection" or "maturity," is highly important to the writer's purpose in this epistle. The writer's use of *teleios* and its cognates are far too numerous to be taken as incidental or without definite design in his argument and scheme.[11] As for the believer's perfection, the concept has to do with becoming mature, moving from the life of an undeveloped child who lacks understanding and the ability to discern, into an advanced stage of the life of godliness (5:12–14). The believer shows maturity when he or she is able to "go on" (6:1) in the Christian life, with no halting because of conflicts and trials. The writer of Hebrews recognized that stages in the life of faith are to be expected, but he insisted, by the steady use of "perfection" terms, that a definite ascent in growth is also expected by means of faith. In his analysis of Hebrews 5:11–6:3, H. P. Owens suggested that the ascent involves grasping the basic instruction in the faith and then the working out of a reasoned pattern of ethical and religious behavior while applying that basic instruction to the daily life.[12] The "perfected" believer (5:14) is the believer whose maturity enables him or her to remain conscious of God's will for their life, and keep fulfilling that will.

---

10. See especially J. Wesley Bready, *England: Before and After Wesley: The Evangelical Revival and Social Reform* (New York and London: Harper & Brothers, 1938).

11. See the writer's use of *teleios* at 5:14; 6:1; 7:11, 19; 9:9, 11; 10:1, 14; 11:22, 40; 12:23.

12. See H. P. Owens, "The 'Stages of Ascent' in Hebrews V.11–VI.3," *New Testament Studies*. Vol. 3, Number 3 (May 1957), pp. 244f. Owens also sees in the author's treatment some correspondence with the schemes of Philo and the Stoics in discussing philosophic childlife. See pp. 244–5.

There is another dimension to the writer's understanding and use of the perfection or maturity concept. Perfection results from companionship with Jesus. Since Jesus has been perfected through testing and now lives as the experienced, holy, triumphant, and exalted Son of God, he has become the one who perfects or brings to maturity those who follow him (5:9). Meanwhile, faith in Jesus procures to the believer the full perfection Jesus has achieved (2:10 with 10:14), "For by a single offering he has perfected for all time those who are sanctified" (10:14). What is already procured for and attributed to the interest of the believer in the sight of God becomes the believer's actualized experience as he or she exercises faith and obedience. In this way the believer's life is continually blessed by the effects of an eternal salvation. Allen Wikgren has written:

> In the application to man or the believer of the idea of
> perfection we have noted that there is an ideal end or goal in
> view. But the very possibility of such a goal depends upon
> a decisive act by which Christ as redemptor and perfector
> is the object of a response of faith by the believer.[13]

Linked with Jesus in an obedience of faith, the believer receives what has been procured to faith, while taking into his or her own experience more and more of what Jesus realized in his life as Son in the world. How altogether crucial, then, for every believer to continue "looking to Jesus the pioneer and perfecter of our faith."

---

13. Allen Wikgren, "Patterns of Perfection in the Epistle to the Hebrews," *New Testament Studies*, vol. 6, no. 2 (January 1960), pp. 161–2. See also the fuller study by David Peterson, *Hebrews and Perfection: An Examination of the Concept of Perfection in the Epistle to the Hebrews* (SNTS Monographs, 47) (Cambridge, England: Cambridge University Press, 1982), especially pp. 174–87.

Chapter 5

The Author's Homiletic

S tirred by his concern to communicate a vital message to help his Christian readers rightly handle their plight and questions occasioned by it, the author of Hebrews prepared and sent them what he, in a personal note appended at the end of the writing, humbly dubbed as "my word of exhortation" (13:22). His description seems intended to cover the entire writing he prepared and his purpose for sending it. The same term is used elsewhere in the New Testament, and it usually describes an extended statement that gives a kerygmatic witness.[1] He asked his readers to "bear with" that word of exhortation, claiming to have "written briefly." His plea seems to imply that he realized his writing could not give the full flavor that a personal speaking visit would have granted.[2]

The writer's hortatory pattern in Hebrews allows us to watch the work of a masterful homilist, a preacher adept in the midrashic style, someone who was intimately familiar with his chosen version of the Hebrew Scriptures (LXX) and experienced in structuring and using rhetoric to share his message with intended effectiveness. His handling of structure, choice of vocabulary, wordplay, illustrative materials, and application strategies

---

1. See Acts 13:15, where the same word is used by the synagogue elders at Pisidian Antioch in inviting Paul and Barnabas to address the group assembled before them if they so desired.

2. It is the view of some, however, that the writer's plea about having "written briefly," or with "few words," should be understood as referring to the more personal materials in chapter 13 and not to the preceding longer section comprising chapters 1–12. See G. A. Simcox, "Heb. xiii; 2 Tim. iv," *Expository Times*, vol. X, 1898–99, p. 386n3.

can teach us much about the importance of form and focus in making sermon content clear, forceful, and engaging. Modem biblical scholarship has called attention to Hebrews as a primary document for tracing the features of early Christian preaching.[3]

In preparing to preach from Hebrews, wisdom for the task is gained by beginning with an in-depth study of the writer's message, on the one hand, seeking an orientation to his hermeneutic system, and then proceeding to an examination of his methods, on the other hand, the rhetorical homiletic he employed to convey that message with such dramatic aliveness. As

---

3. See Lawrence Wills, "The Form of the Sermon in Hellenistic Judaism and Early Christianity," *Harvard Theological Review*, vol. 77:3–4 (1984), especially pp. 277–83. See also a critique of Wills's work in C. Clifton Black II, "The Rhetorical Form of the Hellenistic Jewish and Early Christian Sermon: A Response to Lawrence Wills," *Harvard Theological Review*, vol. 81:1 (1988), pp. 1–18. For those conversant with German, see especially the larger study of Hartwig Thyen, *Der Stil der judischhellenistischen Homilie* (Forschungen zur Religion und Literatur des Alten und Neuen Testaments, No. 47) (GoettingenVandenhoeck & Ruprecht, 1955); James Swetnam's article "On the Literary Genre of the 'Epistle' to the Hebrews" in *Novum Testamentum*, vol. XI, Fasc. 4 (October 1969), pp. 261–69, summarizes, evaluates, and supplements Thyen's study.

The study of the earliest Christian preaching has continued to attract the attention of scholars, and some of them have treated the content and stylistic features within selected examples of the evangelistic preaching of Peter and the missionary preaching by Paul, as reported in the summaries in Acts. The fragmentary character of the biblical reports is evident, but even so one can sense within the accounts the truths, tone, and thrust which characterized the earliest Christian preaching. The Letter to the Hebrews stands out all the more when considered in relation to the brief synopses of preaching as reported in the Acts of the Apostles. Hebrews is an excellent example of a full-scale homily, the longest and most comprehensive in the New Testament. The writer's description of his work as a "word of exhortation" is usually understood as his recognition that it conforms to that rather precise genre common within Hellenistic Judaism and Early Christian groups. The sermons in Acts are fragmentary examples of that genre, while Hebrews is a full-scale example. For an attempted list of fragments of this genre, see Bo Reicke, "A Synopsis of Early Christian Preaching," in *Root of the Vine: Essays in Biblical Theology*, edited by Anton Fridrichsen et al (New York: Philosophical Library, 1953), pp. 128–60.

Joachim Jeremias classified Hebrews not only as a homiletical treatise but as perhaps the oldest Gentile Christian sermon preserved. "Diese alteste uns erhaltene heidenchristliche Predigt (13:22)...." *Der Opfertod Jesu Christi* (Calwer Hefte 62) (StuttgartCalwer Verlag, 1963), p. 5; idem., *The Central Message of the New Testament* (London: SCM Press, Ltd., 1965), p. 31.

Thomas G. Long has explained, "The writers of Scripture faced a communication problem similar to the one encountered by the contemporary preacher—finding the most effective rhetorical shape for their messages."[4] Long went on to suggest that gaining insight into the rhetorical strategies used by a writer of Scripture can be crucial for the right use of the message "packaged" within those forms.[5]

The Writer's Literary Forms and Rhetorical Functions

We have looked at the Letter to the Hebrews in light of the author's purpose, but that preacher's procedure and prowess in pursuing his aim also stand exposed for our admiration, analysis, and instruction. An examination of the literary forms and rhetorical strategies discerned in this epistle reveals that preacher's functional methodology. Hebrews is classified as an epistle, or letter, but it is not a purely formal one. This writing lacks some of the usual epistolary features, such as a formulaic opening that names the sender, the addressees, an offered word of greeting, and a personal statement of good will, although after giving its basic message it does end with a concluding appeal and statement of farewell.[6] For some reason that preacher chose to dispense with the usual introductory formula and began his work with that solemn and stately periodic sentence we find in 1:1–4, a beginning that actually constitutes and artfully states a summary of what is set forth so explicitly in the exhortational writing that follows.

---

4. Thomas G. Long, *Preaching and the Literary Forms of the Bible* (Philadelphia: Fortress Press, 1989), p. 12.

5. Ibid., see especially pp. 43–126.

6. For more about the epistolary format in the New Testament, see J. L. White, *The Body of the Greek Letter* (SBLDS 2) (Missoula, MT: The Scholars Press, 1972); William G. Doty, *Letters in Primitive Christianity* (Philadelphia: Fortress Press, 1973); James L. Bailey and Lyle D. Vander Broek, *Literary Forms in the New Testament: A Handbook* (Louisville: Westminster/John Knox press, 1992) is a helpful examination of the literary forms utilized by Paul, but the treatment of forms in the other New Testament writings, and especially Hebrews, is less extensive.

Several smaller literary forms can be identified throughout the larger epistolary body of Hebrews, along with many evidences of that preacher's rhetorical skills (e.g., paraenesis, exposition, strategic illustrations, figures of speech, alliteration, wordplay, appeal to authority). A selective list of some of those smaller literary and rhetorical forms is given below. This list is not intended to be exhaustive but only illustrative.

1. Admonition: A mild or sharp warning given to bring the reader to a point of reason or reconsideration, by which some danger can be averted or some faulty course of action or behavior corrected.

Examples: Admonition Texts	
2:1–3	12:3
3:12–13	12:15–17
4:1, 11	12:28
5:11–12	13:7
6:11–12	13:13

2. Affirmation: A positive and emphatic assertion of fact or belief that speaks to faith, and always with boldness and confidence.

Examples: Affirmation Texts	
1:1–4	9:24
2:18	9:27–28
4:15	10:14
5:7–9	11:1
7:25	13:8
8:6	13:14

3. Application: The linking of the import of some truth with some hearer's situation and need. An application can be a sentence statement or an extended section that urges the acceptance of what has been stated. Hebrews is filled with application sentences; the writing steadily calls attention to how what has been shared by statement is to be regarded and used, and why it is important to do so. In Hebrews, the writer has given four sections of extended application, each one placed immediately following a section of major teaching. In tracing the relation between the writer's teaching sections and application sections, one can see more clearly the nature and layout of the writer's work.

Teaching Statement	Application Section
1:1–14	2:1–4
2:5–3:6a	3:6b–4:16
5:1–10	5:11–6:20
7:1–10:18	10:19–13:25

4. Appeal to Tradition: The citation of some authoritative person, statement, fact, scripture, or meaning in order to influence the reader's opinion, decision, and stir them to action.

Examples: Appeals to Tradition

1:1

2:3b–4

3:2, 5

9:1–7

5. Commentary: The expansive use of a scriptural quotation, with a focused use of its message, features, or key words to explain a point and apply its meaning. In this epistle we find many examples of the midrashic and pesher style of exegesis used in commentary fashion.

```
+-----------------------------------------------+
|              Examples:                        |
|           Commentary Texts                    |
|                                               |
|    2:6–9       5:5–6       12:5–7             |
|                                               |
|    3:7–19      8:8–13      12:26–27           |
|                                               |
|    4:3–10      10:5–15     13:5–6             |
|                                               |
|                10:36–39                       |
+-----------------------------------------------+
```

6. Biographical Records: Oral or written traditions about some person or group. The use of such traditions is to give evidence of something exemplary or problematic about their life, deeds, influence, and meaning.

```
+-----------------------------------------------+
|              Examples:                        |
|         Biographical Records                  |
|                                               |
|    3:5        5:10        12:3               |
|                                               |
|    3:16–18    6:13        12:12, 16–17       |
|                                               |
|    4:8        7:4–10      12:21              |
|                                               |
|    4:15       7:14        13:12             |
|                                               |
|    5:7        8:5         13:23             |
|                                               |
|             ch. 11 (passim)                   |
+-----------------------------------------------+
```

7. Blessing: A pronouncement prayer-wish that reflects hope and also voices to God some specific concern for the readers. The primary example found in Hebrews of the blessing or prayer-wish form is at 13:20–21. The formal characteristics found in the words of blessing there can be traced as follows:

- an appeal to God ("Now may the God of peace");
- reference to exemplary action on God's part ("who brought back from the dead our Lord Jesus,…);
- stated prayer concern ("make you complete in everything good,…);
- purpose indicated ("so that you may do his will,…);
- ground of hope acknowledged ("through Jesus Christ");
- ascription of praise ("to whom be the glory forever and ever. Amen.").

8. Imperative: An authoritative instruction issued in the interest of some task or behavior.

Examples:
Imperative Texts

13:1–2	13:9
13:3	13:17
13:4	12:14
13:5	12:25

---

9. Example Story: A narrative, biographical record, or brief reference about some person's characteristic trait or deed that shows their nature and disposition to illustrate their wisdom or folly, faith, or failure. The use of the story illustrates some point the writer seeks to make vivid in his argument. For some examples, see the Biographical Records listing.

10. Figurative Speech: Expressive speech that uses metaphors and images in a non-literal sense in order to state or explain some meaning with additional forcefulness and impact.

**Examples:
Figurative Speech**

4:12–13

5:11

5:12b–14

---

11. Hymn: A "song" or poetically structured paean of praise to God or Jesus. The song celebratively states some faith tradition regarding the one being honored and exults about the meaning of that article of faith for the celebrant's life and destiny. Hebrews 1:3–4 shows some formal characteristics of a Christological hymn in (a) metric structure; (b) parallel lines of stress; (c) use of the initial relative pronoun "Who"; and (d) the use of recurring participial phrases.

12. Instruction: Informational material used to teach, persuade, and shape moral behavior and spiritual direction. Hebrews is filled with instructional material.

13. Legend: A story believed to have a basis in history, handed down across generations because of its meaning and import. It is used to instruct, explain, and edify. Hebrews 7:1–10 is based upon a legendary story.

14. Motive Clause: An arousing statement used to stir to belief and prescribed action. It is sometimes allied with a promise and sometimes with a warning.

Examples: Motive Clauses		
3:14	9:13–14	10:39
4:14	9:27–28	12:1–2
4:16	10:10	12:18–24
6:10–12	10:19–22	12:28–29
6:19–20	10:23–25	13:14
7:25	10:35–36	13:16

15. *Paraenesis*: A teaching, or teachings, directed to believers to acquaint with or remind about faith, moral virtues, and motivate to lead a life consistent with the demands of the faith.

```
┌─────────────────────────────────┐
│           Examples:             │
│           Paraenesis            │
│                                 │
│   2:1–4          6:1–8          │
│                                 │
│   2:5–18         10:19–25       │
│                                 │
│   3:12–4:16      12:12–17       │
│                                 │
│   5:7–14         13:1–9         │
│                                 │
│   6:1–2          13:17          │
└─────────────────────────────────┘
```

16. Personal Reflection: A personal consideration or evaluation used to persuade or encourage. A notable example is found at 10:32–34.

17. Rhetorical Question: A question asked for effect so as to highlight an answer that is known and anticipated.

```
┌─────────────────────────────────┐
│           Examples:             │
│      Rhetorical Questions       │
│                                 │
│     1:5         3:17–18         │
│                                 │
│     1:13        12:5            │
│                                 │
│     1:14        12:7            │
│                                 │
│     3:16        12:9b           │
└─────────────────────────────────┘
```

18. Sayings: Authoritative expressions in the form of a proverb, adage, motto, epigram, or scripture text that reflects a principle or promise that guides faith and conduct.

Examples:
Sayings

2:6–8a	10:38
8:12	13:5c
10:30	13:6

19. Summary Appraisal: A statement at the close of a unit to summarize and apply the point of the argument. The appearance of the conclusive use of *therefore* will usually announce a summary sentence and a point of application in this epistle. The instances are numerous.

20. Warning: A pressure statement used to remind or notify of a danger to avoid.

Examples:
Warnings

2:1–4	10:26–31
3:6–4:2	12:15–17
4:11	12:25–29
5:11–6:8	

In summarizing this section, it is necessary to state again that the listing I have supplied here of the writer's literary forms and rhetorical functions is not exhaustive but illustrative. An examination of the verses and sections indicated within the epistle will help one to discern and trace elements of the writer's rhetorical methodology as a preacher.

Indications of the Author's Manner as a Preacher

1. The author of Hebrews was a pastor at heart, and his epistle shows that *he strongly affirmed his identity with his audience.* Among the evidences of this is his repeated use of the collective *we* (41 times, RSV) as he addressed his readers, and his use of *us* (25 times) and *our* (17 times). He used *you* as often as his purpose demanded (50 times), and the possessive *your* occasionally (14 times), but the singular personal pronoun *I* appears only six times (11:32; 13:19 [twice], 22 [twice], 23), unless one also counts that use of a possibly editorial *us* in 13:18, the appearance of *me* in 11:32, and that one use of *my* in 13:22 in referring to his sermon as "my word of exhortation." His steadily inclusive manner of regarding the recipients of this letter-sermon suggests a warmhearted, pastoral person behind this epistle. The tone throughout is one of group awareness and regard for the community.

The author was an affirming leader. Although he dealt frankly with their problems as he knew them—their apparent lack of maturity (5:11–12) and their tempting freedom to "shrink back" under pressures (10:36), among others, he also encouraged the group by recalling for them how they had done well at a crucial time in the past (6:10; 10:32–34). He told them what they were capable of doing and that he trusted them to fulfill his trust and God's trust in them (6:9, 11). He was not a preacher just bent on delivering a message but was eager to affirm a people he loved. He wrote to inspire them to deepened faith and hope.

2. The preacher who wrote Hebrews was *someone determined to be himself and honor his own gifts as he did his work*. The writer was skilled in rhetoric and the art of using words. He wrote with classic style and a cultural alertness. The first sentence of the epistle is a grand periodic sentence that immediately betrays his trained mind, and the rest of the writing only proves his undeniable mastery as both a speaker intent on oral clarity and a writer who wisely wrote for the ear as well as the eye. Throughout Hebrews a musicality is clearly reflected in the preacher's vocabulary, alliteration, wordplay, and steady attentiveness to the very sound of his message.

Arthur John Gossip used to say that "friendship and preaching are alike in that, to make anything of them, you must be your real self...."[7] Gossip therefore advised, "Resolutely you must make up your mind to be yourself, and hold to it. That will involve you in much labour and sore headache, but, in the end, it will bring you into your own natural kingdom and inheritance."[8] The author of Hebrews had entered his own "natural kingdom and inheritance."

3. That preacher was convinced that *the aim of preaching is so important that the best art must be used to serve that aim*. We see this clearly demonstrated in the way he structured his message. The way he framed his sentences, the way he handled his sources, and the way he applied his message at strategic points, these all point to an intentioned approach. The entire epistle is an artistic statement. One wonders what the initial effects were when the recipients heard the group's reader recite the writer's treatment of the heroes and heroines of faith listed in Chapter 11, especially when that richly worded section in verses 32–38 was reached! That whole chapter is grippingly persuasive, and in reading it aloud one realizes anew that effec-

---

7. Arthur John Gossip, *In Christ's Stead: The Warrack Lectures for 1925* (London: Hodder and Stoughton, 1925), pp. 15–16.
8. Ibid., p.17.

tive preaching does not require a lot of words, but just the right ones, rightly related.

4. But central among the many traits this letter evidences about its writer as a preacher is *his understanding and ready use of Scripture.* Hebrews reflects an interpretative procedure allied with a reverent reflection on the Hebrew Scriptures. The writer was intimately acquainted with Israel's ancient texts, and the principal version upon which he depended for his study and his frequent quotations was the Septuagint (LXX).

That preacher's use of Israel's texts and traditions shows how influenced he was in thought and belief by what those texts and traditions report and preserve. The Scriptures stirred his consciousness, and he readily called upon biblical sentences and scenes to express his point, confirm his word, and sustain his authority as spokesman. The writer was first, last, and always biblical, alert to the significations within the texts he cited, and he courageously applied their perceived meaning in declaring the Christian message about the soteric importance of the life and death of Jesus. Convinced that the Hebrew Scriptures are inspired records, that preacher trusted them as a means God uses to mediate a necessary and ever contemporary witness. His treatment of the texts he used shows us his Christological perspective on Jesus as God's Son and the believer's Savior. That preacher's handling of Scripture steadily serves the Christian witness about Jesus as Savior-Son, and the perspective used in discussing Jesus as presently exalted high priest, a view buttressed by an appeal to Psalm 110:4 (109:4, LXX), is unique in the New Testament.

The Focus and Function of Hebrews 11

In the record preserved of some of the "table talk" between Martin Luther and his friend Justus Jonas, there was that time when they talked about Scripture and sermons, about how the preacher must be familiar with each word of the Word in order to declare aright the whole message of the gospel. Yet Luther went on to say, "He that has but one word of God before him, and out of that word cannot make a sermon, can never be a preacher."[9] Judged by what stands before us in Hebrews 11, the writer of Hebrews would have passed Luther's declared test, and grandly, since the contents of that chapter revolves around, and excitingly treats, one word: faith. Perhaps the grandest section in the entire homiletical epistle, chapter 11 is in itself a sermon. Deeply concerned to bless the lives of his readers, and well-skilled in the use of rhetorical devices, the writer chose his illustrative stories and constructed his narrative with a view to shape faith by an appeal to known stalwarts in history. His forceful repetition of "by faith" shows us an artistry put to work in the highest service, the praise of God through the preached word.[10] The oral impact of the writer's anaphoric use of "by faith" is unequalled elsewhere in Scripture, and, read aloud, his unique treatment of the heroes and heroines of faith in Hebrews 11 helps us to reach and realize the deepest level of his message in this epistle.

The writer of Hebrews skillfully informs the reader about what it means to believe, to trust God. Through treating the history of patriarchs and stalwarts, he presents his argument that salvation-history has an ancient origin and that every believer's history connects with that larger history through something other than national heritage, bloodline, historical era, or personal achievement. Thus the writer's emphasis on faith, for faith is the means by which a responsible claim is made upon that salvation which depends upon the gracious action of God. The writer insists that faith in God shapes the best history and that its power to create and sustain is decisive. He urges that faith is the only firm ground on which a person can

---

9. See *The Table Talk of Martin Luther*, edited by Thomas S. Kepler (New York: The World Publishing Co., 1952), p. 8.

10. For a full study of the writer's use of the rhetorical device of anaphora, see Michael R. Cosby, *The Rhetorical Composition and Function of Hebrews 11: In Light of Example Lists in Antiquity* (Macon, GA: Mercer University Press, 1988), especially pp. 41–55.

build a life and gain a truly meaningful future. Every exemplary biographical story he recounts in the chapter illustrates this. At once selective, imaginative, and biblical in his choice of heroes, the writer was also intellectually honest, as when he openly acknowledged the "not yet" aspects of what faith dares to claim and hope rejoices to expect. Hebrews 11 tells us what it is, and what it means, to be a Christian pilgrim, to be someone in process, someone moving through life with a sense of purpose, eyes cast forward intent to see and reach an expected goal. Hebrews 11 gives us an example series in celebration of the power of faith, and all the biographical characters fall into the positive category. Later, however, in the next chapter, a negative example is cited (Esau, 12:16–17) to warn that undisciplined living also brings its returns.

Chapter 6:

Preaching from Hebrews

The preparation of sermons based on texts in Hebrews requires the same approach in handling other biblical texts. The right and effective use of a text must be preceded by a right understanding of it, so one must begin with biblical-theological concerns about the textual message, the contextual setting of that message, the truth served by the text, and the functional thrust of that truth in one's own contemporary setting. The biblical-homiletical concern then follows, so that ancient text is addressed to the contemporary situation with due meaning, clarifying perspective, and engaging expression.

Hermeneutical Guidelines for Preaching From Hebrews

1. Determine the boundaries of the textual unit being examined for use.

Exegetical and hermeneutical work proceeds best when a basic sense unit has been isolated for detailed study. The most basic and simplest sense unit in Scripture is the sentence. The sentence can be a self-contained unit of thought that makes sense even after being isolated from its original context, or it can be a pivotal section within a larger structured unit whose pattern of words demands that it remain connected; but whether a sentence is handled as a single unit or kept related to a larger section, the entire unit must hold a self-contained message in order to provide the best foundation for a sermon.

The sentences in Hebrews demand considerable attention for use in preaching. This is partly because the writer's argument is so closely woven across the entire epistle and partly because his sentences are so often complex in structure. The writer's usage of Greek is poetic at many places, and his calculated use of word order and clustered phrasing in developing cadences to highlight his emphases calls for some ability on the part of the exegete to unpack his sentences. Translators who have worked from the Greek text of Hebrews have done considerable service in rendering the many periodic sentences of the author into current English usage. For example, Hebrews 1:1–4, which is one sentence in Greek, was rendered as three sentences in the New Revised Standard Version. Hebrews 2:2–4 is another long sentence in Greek that was rendered as two in the NRSV. There are many long sentences in the Greek text of Hebrews, but this is not readily evident in the many English renderings of the epistle that are presently available.[1]

There are some simple sentences in Hebrews, many of which are of declarative importance for preaching, sentence units such as at 4:12, 15, 16, or 13:8, to name but a few, but there are also many compound and compound-complex sentences with which the preacher will have to wrestle in determining a focal boundary for concise handling in the pulpit.

Admittedly, Hebrews is a difficult book from which to preach. Dwight E. Stevenson, who always encouraged preachers to benefit their churches through more Bible-based preaching, listed Hebrews at the top of his list of the twelve most difficult books of the New Testament, and as the hardest book among them from which to preach.[2]

The lengthy and involved argument presented in Hebrews does not yield readily to an easy break-down for sermonizing, and many blocks of

---

1. See, among others, in the Greek New Testament, the following sentences: 2:8–9, 14–15; 3:12–15; 4:12–13; 5:1–3, 7–10; 6:4–6, 16–10; 7:1–3; 8:4–6; 9:2–5, 6–10, 24–26; 10:11–13, 19–25; 11:24–26; 12:1–2, 18–24. See also James Moffatt, *A Critical and Exegetical Commentary on the Epistle to the Hebrews* (The International Critical Commentary) (Edinburgh, Scotland T. & T. Clark, 1924), pp. lvi–lxiv.

2. See Dwight E. Stevenson, *Preaching on the Books of the New Testament* (New York: Harper & Brothers, 1956), p. 17.

material deal with the same aspect of thought, although ascensively. Some preachers have sought to deal with such difficulties by isolating texts that can be addressed to life without special regard for their original setting or context. They discerned an apt sense-boundary that served their pulpit interest well.

George A. Buttrick (1892–1980) in his *Sermons Preached in a University Church* published two sermons based on texts drawn from Hebrews. Buttrick used 4:12–13 to deal with the theme "God and Our Mixed Motives," and from Hebrews 11:13, 16 he developed a sermon about "Frustration and Faith."[3] The last sermon in Aaron N. Meckel's volume of sermons, *Living Can Be Exciting,* is a treatment of Hebrews 2:15, titled "Why Fear Death."[4] In his *The Greatest Texts of the Bible,* Clarence Edward Macartney's (1879–1957) sermon based on 12:1, "The Sin Which Doth Beset Us," appears and also an instructive sermon on that classic verse at 13:8, "The Same Yesterday, Today, Forever."[5] *Preaching on Controversial Issues,* which Harold A. Bosley wrote and published during the mid-twentieth century, contains nineteen sermons about "living issues for our generation." One of those sermons concerns "The Faith That Strengthens," based on Hebrews 11:32–12:4.[6] Among several excellently crafted sermons by Arthur Leonard Griffith in his *What Is A Christian?* are three lively treatments of texts from Hebrews: "Drifting Away From Reality" (2:1–4), "Refusing to Grow Up" (6:1), and "The Pilgrim View of Life" (11:13).[7]

---

3. George Arthur Buttrick, *Sermons Preached in a University Church* (Nashville, TN: Abingdon Press, 1959), see pp. 103–9 and 110–16, respectively.

4. Aaron N. Meckel, *Living Can Be Exciting* (New York: E. P. Dutton and Co., Inc., 1956), see pp. 239–50.

5. Clarence Edward Macartney, *The Greatest Texts of the Bible* (Nashville, TN: Abingdon-Cokesbury Press, 1947), see pp. 160–70 and 183–95, respectively.

6. See Harold A. Bosley, *Preaching on Controversial Issues* (New York: Harper & Brothers, 1953), especially pp. 36–43.

7. A. Leonard Griffith, *What Is a Christian?* (Nashville, TN: Abingdon Press, 1962), see pp. 193–203, 204–13, and 214–23, respectively.

The texts most frequently used in preaching from Hebrews have been those drawn from chapter 11, probably because the biographical data there can be adapted more readily to pulpit use, and the text boundaries in that chapter are easier to isolate for sermons. Given that the central message of Hebrews is about the significance of Jesus, however, one would expect the sermonic literature to contain more sermons from texts in Hebrews that highlight this emphatic message. Englishman Frederick William Robertson (1816–1853), of Brighton, sensed the importance of Hebrews in this regard. Two sermons of his must be cited in particular: one based on 1:1–2, titled "Christ the Son," and the other based on 4:15–16, titled "The Sympathy of Christ."[8] .Harry Emerson Fosdick (1878–1969) preached a topical treatment of Hebrews 2:8–9, titled "Christ Himself Is Christianity," that is worthy of study, and so is that classic sermon of John Albert Broadus (1827–1895) on Hebrews. 7:25, titled "He Ever Liveth to Intercede."[9]

Gardner C. Taylor's sermon on "The Christian's Dearest Sight," based on Hebrews 2:9, kept the central message of Hebrews in clear view. Hebrews 2:9 is a sense unit whose message pointedly culminates that sectional portion of the writer's argument about the exemplary life of Jesus. Verse 2:9 runs as follows: "but we do see Jesus, who for a little while was made lower than the angels, now crowned with glory and honor because of the suffering of death, so that by the grace of God he might taste death for everyone." Taylor used the text to celebrate Jesus as the most treasured view available

---

8. Frederick William Robertson, *Sermons Preached at Brighton* (New York: Harper and Brothers, 1947), see pp. 88–98 and 327–33, respectively.

9. See Harry Emerson Fosdick, "Christ Himself Is Christianity," in *Best Sermons: 1947–1948*, edited by G. Paul Butler (New York: Harper & Brothers, 1947), see pp. 2–7.; John A. Broadus, *Favorite Sermons of John A. Broadus*, edited by Vernon L. Stanfield (New York: Harper and Brothers, 1959), pp. 28–37.

to faith now, and to our full sight later, and what this means for life as we know it.[10] Taylor structured the sermon by a four-part design:

I. *The dearest sight a Christian can ever have is Jesus.*
    A. He is the express image of God
    B. He is the clearest vision we can have of the divine nature.

II. *The sight of Jesus helps us to endure what is not yet right about life as we know it.*
    A. He helps us endure human failure.
    B. He helps us endure human frailty.
    C. He is our clue to how things shall be.

III. *The sight of Jesus gives us a new understanding of our role in life.*

IV. *We shall not see Jesus fully here, but later we shall see him as he really is.*

In his statement about Jesus being "the express image of God," Taylor was following the writer's textual message in Hebrews 1:3–4, seeking to link the message about Jesus from an earlier part of the epistle with the conclusive statement text about Jesus in 2:9. Having studied the unit, Taylor decided to isolate it as a basic statement to be expounded and applied.

The writer's assertion that "but we do see Jesus" (2:9) emphasizes a central insight in his theological message, and Taylor, influenced by the African American contemplative way of reading the Scriptures, did not miss that insight. Like the writer of Hebrews, Taylor knew that "seeing" Jesus is experienced in more than one way. At Heb 3:1–6, a passage that is an artful blend of history, theology, and doctrine, the writer exhorts the reader to "consider [*katanoesate* 3:1] Jesus," meaning to "fix the mind upon" him, and at 12:2 he stresses the need to keep "looking [*aphorontes*] to

---

10. Gardner C. Taylor, *The Scarlet Thread: Nineteen Sermons* (Elgin, IL: Progressive Baptist Publishing House, 1981), pp. 136–50. The sermon appears also in *The Words of Gardner Taylor*, vol. 2, compiled by Edward L. Taylor (Valley Forge: Judson Press, 2000), see pp. 72–77.

Jesus." That emphasis upon "seeing" Jesus and "looking to" Jesus takes the New Testament tradition of seeing the Lord to another level. The writer does not refer to seeing Jesus by normal vision blessed with an objective appearance, such as the twelve disciples experienced, who met with the risen Lord and afterward confessed, "We have seen the Lord" (John 20:25).

Our writer rather refers to sight of another kind, namely insight, a spiritual perception by which the believer is actively influenced by, and identifies with, Jesus. This kind of seeing is a grace-assisted understanding of who Jesus is, and it includes a realization of the personal benefits Jesus makes available in the believer's experience. "Seeing" Jesus has occurred, and still occurs, in more than one way.

Near the close of that sermon, Gardner Taylor mentioned having preached one night, early in his ministry, in Shreveport, Louisiana, when at some point during his delivery the lights in that section of the city failed and the church was plunged into darkness. Startled momentarily, Taylor stopped preaching; but a voice soon rang out from one of the pews, "Go on, Preacher; we can see Jesus in the darkness." Seeing Jesus is experienced in more than one way, and each way is a meaningful experience.

Arthur John Gossip (1873–1954), the Scottish pulpit master, used the same text for his sermon "On the Clue to Life's Enigmas."[11] Calling attention both to the context of the passage and the times of his hearers, Gossip began with these words: "Life was not easy to this writer; and, even with his gloriously valiant faith to help him, he never pretended that it was." He continued, "There are mysteries that haunt, and enigmas that confuse and shake the soul, and dark, tremendous facts that must be faced and taken into full account in our reading of things."[12] Aware that most persons are bothered by their "reading of things," and feel "stunned and staggered

---

11. Arthur John Gossip, *The Hero in Thy Soul* (New York: Charles Scribner's Sons, 1929), pp. 117–29.
12. Ibid., p. 117.

and reeling in mind," Gossip used the text to help his hearers deal with dark and grey days, urging them to see and understand Jesus as "the clue, the key, the motive in God's mind, aye, and the power that will work out His plans to glorious realities."[13] The sermon outline is not obvious—few of Gossip's sermon outlines are—but although his thought is tight and pithy, his message was vital, always moving the hearer forward to see that what God has done and is doing in Jesus remains for us the basis for real hope and a ready help. Both Gossip and Taylor preached to inspire in their hearers a confidence to "approach the throne of grace with boldness," so as to "receive mercy and find grace to help in time of need" (Heb 4:16).

Harry Emerson Fosdick, in his sermon "Christ Himself Is Christianity," mentioned above, used Hebrews 2:8–9 from another angle of emphasis at Christmastime. The sermon had four points:

1. The coming of Jesus was prophetic.

2. The coming of Jesus was historically influential.

3. The coming of Jesus was personally moving.

4. The coming of Jesus is a reassuring fact.

Fosdick prepared and delivered that sermon when America and the Western world were suffering from postwar disillusionment. He used the text to speak helpfully to those who were confused and fretful about the world and conditions they had inherited.

---

13. Ibid., p. 122.

2. Locate and compare other texts in the letter that complement your textual unit to gain a full view of what your chosen preaching unit treats.

This principle is important in handling the verses and message in Hebrews because of the writer's constancy of theme, his strategically used focal terms, his referential dependence upon several Old Testament texts, and the spiral approach he uses in restating himself for emphasis. Having dealt with the writer's theme and the structure of his work, attention will now be given to the focal terms he used and to the intertextuality upon which so much in Hebrews depends.[14]

A. TEXTS USING COMPLEMENTARY FOCAL TERMS

Within the well-stocked vocabulary used by the author of Hebrews, and central to his argument, were several focal terms. The texts in which those terms appear should be studied in relation to each other in order to see parallels, their combined focus, or any possible contrasts between them in the way the terms are used. An alphabetical listing of some of the writer's focal terms is given below, with locations in the epistle.

I. *"age(s)"*
    A. *aion.* 1:2, 8; 5:6; 6:5, 20; 7:17, 21, 24, 28; 9:26; 11:3; 13:8, 21.
    B. [eternal] *aionios.* 5:9; 6:2; 9:12, 14, 15; 13:20
II. *"better"*
    A. *kreitton.* 1:4; 6:9; 7:7, 19.22; 8:6; 9:23; 10:34; 11:16, 35, 40; 12:24
III. *"confession"*
    A. *homologeo.* 11:13; 13:15
    B. *homologia.* 3:1; 4:14; 10:23

---

14. On the subject of intertextuality in Hebrews, see Sean Freyne, "Reading Hebrews and Revelation Intertextually," in *Intertextuality in Biblical Writings: Essays in Honour of Bas van Iersel,* edited by Sipke Draisma (Kampen, Netherlands: Uitgeversmaatschappi J. H. Kok, 1989), pp. 83–93.

IV. *"confidence"*

    A.   *parrhesia.* 3:6; 4:16; 10:19, 35

    B.   *hupostasis.* 1:3; 3:14; 11:1

V. *"covenant"*

    A.   *diatheke.* 7:22; 8:6, 8, 9, 10; 9:4, 15, 16, 17, 20; 10:16, 29; 12:24; 13:20

VI. *"enlightened"*

    A.   *photizo.* 6:4; 10:32

VII. *"faith"*

    A.   *pisteuo.* 4:3; 11:6

    B.   *pistis.* 4:2; 6:1, 12; 10:22, 38, 39; 11:1, 3, 4, 5, 6, 7, 8, 9, 11, 13, 17, 20, 21, 22, 23, 27, 28, 29, 30, 31, 33, 39; 12:2; 13:7

    C.   *pistos.* 2:17; 3:2, 5; 10:23; 11:11

VIII. *"fall away"*

    A.   *parapipto.* 6:6

    B.   *pipto.* 3:17; 4:11; 11:30

IX. *"great(er)"*

    A.   *megas.* 4:14; 10:35; 13:20

    B.   *meizon.* 6:13, 16; 9:11; 11:26

    C.   [degree] *pelikos.* 7:4

    D.   *telikoutos. 2:3*

    E.   [quantity] *tosoutos.* 121

X. *"heaven[ly/s]"*

    A.   *epouranios.* 3:1; 6:4; 8:5; 9:23; 11:16; 12:22

    B.   *ouranos.* 1:10; 4:14; 7:26; 8:1; 9:23, 24; 11:12; 12:23, 25, 26

XI. *"holiness"*

    A.   *hagiazmos.* 12:14

    B.   [sanctify] *hagiazo.* 2:11; 9:13; 10:10, 14, 29

    C.   [holy] *hagios.* 3:1; 6:4, 10; 10:15; 13:24

XII. *"hope"*

    A.   *elpizo.* 11:1

    B.   *elpis.* 3:4; 6:11, 18; 7:19; 10:23

XIII. *"Jesus"*

    A.   *Iesous.* 2:9; 3:1; 4:14; 6:20; 7:22; 10:19; 12:2, 24; 13:12, 20

    B.   [with *Christos*]. 3:1; 10:10; 13:8, 21

    C.   [*Christos* alone]. 3:6, 14; 5:5; 6:1; 9:11, 14, 24, 28; 11:26

XIV. *"Judge"*

    A.   *krites.* 12:23

XV. *"Judgment"*

    A.   *krimatos.* 6:2

    B.   *krisis.* 9:27; 10:27

    C.   *krino.* 10:30; 13:4

XVI. *"Perfect(ion)"*

    A.   *teleios.* 5:14; 9:11

    B.   *teleiotes.* 61

    C.   *teleioo.* 2:10; 5:9; 7:19, 28; 9:9; 10:1, 14; 11:40; 12:23

    D.   *teleiosis.* 711

    E.   *teleutao. 11:22*

XVII. *"Priest(hood)"*

    A.   *hiereus.* 5:6; 7:1, 3, 11, 14, 15, 17, 20, 21, 23; 8:4; 9:6; 10:11, 21

    B.   ["High Priest"] *archiereus.* 2:17; 3:1; 4:14, 15; 5:1, 5, 10; 6:20; 7:26, 27, 28; 8:1, 3; 9:7, 11, 25; 10:11; 13:11

XVIII. *"Promise"*

    A.   *epaggella.* 4:1; 6:12, 15, 17; 7:6; 8:6; 9:15; 10:36; 11:9, 13, 17, 33, 39

    B.   *epaggello.* 6:13; 10:23; 11:11; 12:26

XIX. *"Rest"*

    A.   *katapausis.* 3:11,18; 4:1, 3, 5, 10, 11

    B.   *katapauo.* 4:4, 8, 10

XX. *"Righteous(ness)"*

    A.   *dikaiosune.* 1:9; 5:13; 7:2; 11:7, 33, 12:11

    B.   *euthutes.* 18

XXI. *"Sacrifice"*

    A.   *thusia.* 5:1; 7:27; 8:3; 9:9, 23, 26; 10:1, 5, 8, 11, 12, 26; 11:4; 13:15, 16.

    B.   *thusiasterion.* 7:13; 13:10

XXII. *"Seated"*

    A.   *kathemai.* 113

    B.   *kathizo.* 1:3; 8:1; 10:12; 12:2

    C.   *kathistemi.* 2:7; 5:1; 7:28; 8:3

XXIII. *"Sin"*

    A.   *hamartano.* 317; 10:26;

    B.   *hamartia.* 1:3; 2:17; 3:13; 4:15; 5:1, 3; 7:27; 8:12; 9:26,28; 10:2, 3, 4, 6, 8, 11, 12, 17, 18, 26; 11:25; 12:1,4; 13:11

    C.   *hamartolos.* 7:26; 12:3.

XXIV. *"Son(s)"*

    A.   [Jesus] *huios.* : 1:2, 5, 8; 3:6; 4:14; 5:5, 8; 6:6; 7:3, 28; 10:29.

    B.   [believers] 2:6, 10; 7:5; 11:21, 22, 24; 12:5, 6, 7, 8.

XXV. *"Temptation"*

    A.   *peirazo.* 2:18; 3:9; 4:15; 11:17;

    B.   *peirasmos. 3:8.*

XXVI. *"Worship"* / Serve God

    A.   *latreia.* 9:1, 6

    B.   *latreuo.* 8:5; 9:9, 14; 10:2; 12:28; 1310

    C.   *proskuneo.* 1:6; 11:21

B. Other Features in the Writer's Use of Texts

The quest for a fullness of view regarding the message of Hebrews depends as well upon understanding how the writer used Old Testament texts and accounts about Israel's revered figures. His letter could not exist without previous texts, nor can it be understood apart from those texts. For example, in declaring, "Now faith is the assurance of things hoped for, the conviction of things not seen" (11:1), the writer moved immediately from propositional statement to a confirmation of data from previous texts of scripture to an instance its truthfulness. It was not enough to declare his point; he was intent to make that point, and he did so by citing known and contagious accounts about persons mentioned in the Hebrew Scriptures whose illustrative lives exemplified the results of faith.

Throughout Hebrews, the writer maintains a strict association between his distinctive plan and the ancient stories and texts he selected to serve the purpose behind his plan. He used a recital scheme that teaches, reminds, and inspires by its controlled perspective. He had assessed biblical history and had gained some treasured insights about the ways of God with his people, and those insights blessed his approach as he wrote, giving focus to his mention of divine commands, human responses, crucial periods, scriptural statements, and focal persons.

The use of earlier texts was important to his recital approach, and his appeal to history tapped interest levels that propositions and declarations alone might have left untouched. Actually, reading Hebrews can help a preacher learn how to respond to texts, gain perspective from them, appropriate their message, and be stirred to share that message with others.

The writer's concise way of retelling the known accounts reported in Hebrews 11 shows his creativity in grand focus. His was no mere historicist approach to the Scriptures; his engagement with the Septuagint was such that he went beyond giving attention only to what *was,* and was prepared to use it to deal aptly with what *is*. He worked to provide guidance at the very points where his readers were experiencing tension in their lives. He knew the purpose of preaching and the resources essential to his work. He did not force any compliance between that upon which he drew and the point he wished to make. He did not arbitrarily subject texts and stories to his plan; he rather surrendered himself to the perspective he gained from his sources, which readied him to share their meaning and effects within the setting he had to address. He knew the *What* (sense) provided in the Hebrew Scriptures (LXX), so he was determined to deal with the *So what?* (significance), the applicability of that *What* to his hearers' needs. There is much to be learned from the Letter to the Hebrews about how the biblical tradition can be used in new settings and with fresh perspective. And gaining a fullness of view about what a text treats, and why, is crucial to this end.

3. Study the "perspective" in the text to see what is highlighted to be understood, received, and done.

Every basic sense unit in Scripture offers its perspective by which some particular element of meaning is highlighted. A dictionary definition of *perspective* traces the word back to the Latin *perspicere,* which means to "look through." It is an optical term that describes how something is viewed in relation to other things around it. Competent artists are skilled in picturing figures and objects and scenes in perspective, in treating background and foreground with such attentiveness that what should be close remains close and distinct from what should be understood as distant. Using lines and space, lights and shadows, those artists enhance and highlight one thing in the midst of other things. The music of great composers remains special because of their mastery of perspective. A listener can marvel at the contrapuntal intricacies of J. S. Bach's *Goldberg Variations,* over how he blended art and technology, and yet can understandably follow the theme because he kept one musical line in the pattern highlighted in the midst of several other lines. Competent writers also distinguish between things, and they highlight some offered insight through the strategic use of words.

The literary excellence of Hebrews is an acknowledged fact, and those who read Hebrews are helped by the writer's skill to "see" the meaning of Old Testament history in perspective. The historical references and scriptural quotations and focal terms in the letter help the reader to look through and view salvation–history with sharper focus and an increased depth of understanding. Scotsman George A. Gordon (1853–1929) expressed the matter quite pointedly not only for Hebrews but for the total canon of the Scriptures when he wrote:

> Since the Bible has its chief value as a witness to the Eternal, the approach to what is central in that witness, whether historical or human, should be in the vision of a sound perspective.[15]

The perspective offered in each sense unit of Hebrews is better understood when seen in relation to the main argument of the letter, after repeated readings and depth study have yielded what Ludwig Wittgenstein referred to in another connection as "aspect perception."[16] Examining the writer's focal terms, and understanding the structure of the letter can greatly assist the preacher to gain that aspect perception. Gardner C. Taylor's aspect perception homework on Hebrews 2:9 is clearly seen in his sermon on "The Christian's Dearest Sight." Arthur Gossip's understanding of that text is also evident in his "The Clue to Life's Enigmas." Both Taylor and Gossip saw what that unit pointed out to them, and they highlighted its message with faith and fresh-

---

15. George A. Gordon, "Some Things Worth While in Theology," *Harvard Theological Review*, vol. 3, no. 4 (October 1910), p. 378.

16. See Ludwig Wittgenstein, *Philosophical Investigations* (Oxford, England: Basil Blackwell, 1953), p. 193 c.

ness. George A. Buttrick's aspect perception regarding Hebrews 11:13, 16, is readily sensed in his sermon on "Frustration and Faith." Buttrick applauded the "stark realism" of the writer of Hebrews, knowing, as that writer knew, that "the promises and hopes of our mortal days are not fulfilled," and that "We die with half our music in us."[17] Centering attention on three pivotal terms, Buttrick declared "Three words preside over our life—promise, faith, and frustration."[18] "So what to do?" He answered that life must be viewed through the eyes of faith even as we work through the frustrations that life presents. According to his outline:

1. We must not deny the frustration.

2. We must not deny the promise faith.

3. We can accept the frustration and handle it in faith, letting Jesus— who bore a Cross—show us how.

4. Those who keep faith meet God and experience a "life beyond this life."

4. Personally appropriate the message of the text and prayerfully refocus its insight with your projected hearers in mind.

The personal appropriation of a text includes more than an acknowledgment of its importance as part of the given canon; it involves opening the self to the truth and claim the text presents. The appropriation is made personal as the text is honored within the heart as the word of God to the self. Thomas H. Troeger was pointing to this when he wrote:

---

17. George Arthur Buttrick, *Sermons Preached in a University Church* (Nashville, TN: Abingdon Press, 1959), p. 110.
18. Ibid., p. 112.

Before they consult any commentaries or other Bible aids, the first thing preachers need to do is immerse themselves in the text, not in order to figure out what to say to others, but in order to hear what God has to say to them. Preachers cannot expect to change the listener's heart and soul and mind and strength when their own have not been touched.[19]

Appropriating a text happens best when it is "received" as God's word, when it is heard and accepted, when the preacher is humbly claimed by it, so that the text holds priority and is not subjected to the preacher's control. Joachim Jeremias (1900–1979) was known to advise that "those who carry on the ministry of the Word" must not read into the biblical text what he or she would like to find there." "Exegesis," he insisted, "is, after all, a matter of obedience."[20] He was speaking of obedience to the meaning indicated in the text and of obedience to the God who inspired Scripture.

The message in the biblical text should be received personally before it is handled professionally. That "receiving" requires something more than purely natural abilities, Paul instructed, because "Those who are unspiritual *psuchikos,* 'natural,' do not receive the gifts of God's Spirit, for they are foolishness to them, and they are unable to understand them because they are spiritually discerned" (1 Cor 2:14). The favorable reception of a word from God is aided by God's Spirit, but it requires our openness to be aided. Interest-

---

19. Thomas H. Troeger, "Shaping Sermons by the Encounter of Text with Preacher," in *Preaching Biblically: Creating Sermons in the Shape of Scripture*, edited by Don M. Wardlaw (Philadelphia: Westminster Press, 1983), p. 155.

20. Joachim Jeremias, *The Eucharistic Words of Jesus* (London: SCM Press, Ltd., 1966), p. 8. Eng. trans. by Norman Perrin. After Jeremias died in 1979, Eduard Lohse commented in a memorial article about him that "as a teacher he awakened joy in the study of theology in many students, and he taught more than two generations of pastors to interpret Biblical texts with methodically trained conscientiousness." See "Joachim Jeremias in memoriam," *Zeitschrift fur die Neutestamentliche Wissenschaft*, 70 Band 1979, Heft 3/4, p. 140.

ingly, in his statement about "receiving," Paul was careful to use the word *dechomai,* which implies an appreciative reception of something or the welcoming of someone; He did not use *lambano,* which also means to receive, but often with the sense of seizing or controlling something.[21]

The biblical text is given, it is fixed, it is foundational for faith, but it's message must be spiritually received for any fullness of meaning to be appropriated and handled without any constricting control over the text. On this matter of control, there are sections in Hebrews where the writer has used quotations from the Old Testament (Greek Septuagint, LXX) in ways that appear to be controlling. His use of Psalm 40:6–8 (39:7–9a, LXX) at Hebrews 10:5–7 is one such section. Observe how he took Psalm 40:6b, which reads, "But you have given me an open ear," and changed the line to read "but a body *[soma]* you have prepared for me" (Heb 10:5b). This is not the place to deal with the difficulties those who prepared the Septuagint sometimes had in carrying Hebrew meanings over into translation Greek, but it must be noted that a direct equivalence was not achieved in translating Psalm 40:6b from the Hebrew Masoretic Text. The line in that text runs: "ears *[oznayim]* you have dug for me" The equivalent term for "ears" in Greek is *otia,* but the Greek-speaking translators used *soma,* which means "body," which seems out of character. Whether or not the writer of Hebrews was at home in the Hebrew language is not clear, but in quoting his source, he wrote the LXX rendering, *but not verbatim:* He abbreviated and truncated that Psalm section. He credited the words to Christ and changed the statement "I delight to do your will" (Ps 40:8), which was spoken to God, to read, "I have come to do your will" (Heb 10:7a). While we cannot be certain that the writer was quoting from the same Greek version of the Psalms that has been transmitted to us, what-

---

21. See *Mounce's Complete Expository Dictionary of Old & New Testament Words,* edited by William D. Mounce (Grand Rapids, MI: Zondervan, 2006), especially pp. 563–64, 704–5.

ever that version was, his messianic interpretation of its rendering of that psalm influenced his handling of that text. Commentator William Lane commented that "The words of the Old Testament are quoted [by that writer] not for their significance in the past but rather for their significance in the present."[22] His interest was to use that text illustratively, supportively, prophetically, and pastorally. While his use of that text presents problems when compared with the careful research exacted of us for preaching in our time, his handling of those verses imposed no constraining control over the text, and that handling did not skew the meaning of the text. The meaning of that text was still controlling the writer's thought as he sharpened its application to address people needing his word in a new setting and situation.

It needs to be said that the writer's way of handling the Scriptures was not unique. The typological treatment of Scripture was a current and common exegetical method in the church during that time.[23] The entire Letter to the Hebrews is an example of early Christian exegesis about the meaning of the cross of Christ, but the methodology utilized to expose and apply that meaning was not unique to our author. The use of a place, event, ritual, person, and so on, as a type [*tupos,* "pattern," "model," "example," "scheme"] was understood, exegetically, as a parallel example, with the earlier one prefiguring the later and greater one. This method of interpreting Scripture on the basis of the principle of correspondence lead to a point of view for considering a matter. The point was to arrive at a needed understanding of the present in relation to some-

---

22. See William Lane, *Hebrews*, vol 1 (Word Biblical Commentary, No. 47A) (Dallas: Word Books, Publisher, 1991).

23. On this. see Leonard Goppelt, *Typos: The Typologcal Interpretation of the Old Testament in the New* (Grand Rapids, MI: Wm. B. Eerdmans Publishing Co., 1He2), especially pp. 161–78. Eng. trans. by Donald H. Madvig. See also Anthony T. Hanson, "Hebrews," in *It Is Written: Scripture Citing Scripture, Essays in Honour of Barnabas Lindars*, edited by D. A. Carson and H. G. M. Williamson (Cambridge, England: Cambridge University Press, 1988).

thing or someone in the past. Typological exegesis is not a purely arbitrary system. It is rooted in the human concern to see basic relationships, and it honors history and historical process. It is based on the human bent to think analogically. Believing that new persons and events could be appreciated more adequately and understood more fully in terms of previous persons and events mentioned in the Scriptures, the writer of Hebrews used typology to open to his readers a new level of realization of the will and ways of God. His insightful treatment has given Christians insight into the dynamic continuity between God's dealings in the past and his action in the present, as well as faith in God's promised future action. With respect to that writer's use of typology in interpreting Scripture, Anthony T. Hanson commented that he was "a very able and imaginative exegete," who "sets out to interpret the work of Christ in terms of the *cultus* as recorded in Scripture; in this he is remarkably successful." Hanson added:

> Both in his clear indication of what is obsolete, and in his Christianized use of scriptural terms, his work has been of the greatest value to the Christian Church down through the ages. If indeed the theologians of the early Middle Ages in the West had paid more attention to his theology they would have avoided much unsatisfactory exposition of the significance of Christ's sacrifice.[24]

This, too, must be said about the writer's use of that text from Psalm 40: even if he knew Hebrew and had quoted the Hebrew line "ears you have dug for me" (MT Ps 40:7b), his Christological interpretation of it would still have been apt. The expression "opened ears" (Greek) or "bored ears" (Hebrew) equates with "pierced ears," and the allusion is to Exodus 21:2–6

---

24. Anthony T. Hanson, "Hebrews," in *It Is Written: Scripture Citing Scripture, Essays in Honour of Barnabas Lindars*, edited by D. A. Carson and H. G. M. Williamson (Cambridge, England: Cambridge University Press, 1988), p. 300.

and Deuteronomy 15:12–17 where the conditions are stated for bond-servants to gain their freedom.[25] According to Ex. 21:5–6, an indentured male Hebrew who worked for six years to pay off an outstanding debt was free to leave his master's household in the seventh year. If that master and servant had developed such relations that the servant wished to remain in his master's employ, then the servant could become a permanent part of the household through a formal ceremony. After declaring his intention to his master, the two of them would announce it to the sanctuary leaders (or the city magistrates). Next:

> He shall be brought to the door or the doorpost; and his master shall pierce his ear with an awl; and he shall serve him for life. (Ex 21:6)[26]

The pierced ear symbolized that person's submission, on the one hand, and his permanent status, on the other. Wearing a ring in the pierced ear would be in recognition of the relationship thus established. When the writer of Hebrews used the words "a body you have prepared for me" and linked those words with Christ's voluntary incarnation, he thereby highlighted that same theme of submission (Jesus') to God's will and also

---

25. Some scholars suggest that the expression about an "opened [or bored] ear" should be understood to mean the willingness of a person who has heard God's command to obey it, since "the instruments for obedience, the ears, were made by God (cf. Psalm 94:9; 'He who planted the ear ...')." Walter C. Kaiser, Jr., *The Uses of the Old Testament in the New* (Chicago: Moody Press, 1985), p. 134. The ears thus represent the total person. For an additional treatment of the textual and lexical issues interfaced in Hebrews 10:5–7, see Karen H. Jobes and Moises Silva, *Invitation to the Septuagint* (Grand Rapids, MI: Baker Academic, 2000), especially pp. 195–98; Gleason L. Archer and Gregory Chirichigno, *Old Testament Quotations in the New Testament* (Chicago: Moody Press, 1983).

26. On the Exodus 2:1–6 passage, see John I. Durham, *Exodus* (Word Biblical Commentary, no. 3) (Waco, TX: Word Books, 1987), p. 321. On the Deuteronomy 15:12–17 passage, see Ronald E. Clements, "The Book of Deuteronomy: Introduction, Commentary, and Reflections," *New Interpreter's Bible*, vol. 2 (Nashville, TN: Abingdon Press, 1998), p. 405.

called attention to how Jesus offered his body (himself) to make believers acceptable to God (10:10).

The Psalm 40:6–8 text was one of the writer's most important witnesses, or evidences, as he sought to explain why the old order of sacrifices had to be abolished. Like Psalms 50, 51, and 69, all of which clearly state that God desires something more from humans than sacrificed animals, Psalm 40 held the same message, but in addition it offered the very *words* needed to highlight Jesus as the perfect self-offering who has made the old order of sacrifices no longer necessary (Heb 10:9–10).

Although problematic at points, the writer's dependence upon the Septuagint (LXX) was practical—and just as expected as any preacher's steady dependence upon any authorized version or translation in our own day! Problematic, in how that Greek version differs at points from the parent text of Hebrew Scriptures it was produced to render; but practical, indeed, in that it was the Bible the writer and his readers knew. Expressions and words of the Septuagint were so indelibly fixed in their minds that, as one historian put it, "without it the religion of the Greek-speaking Jews was as unthinkable as the Church of England without the Authorized Version."[27] Since the early part of the third century BC, the LXX had become a normal part of the synagogue life and liturgy of Greek-speaking Jews. The LXX was the accepted translated Scriptures in the first century AD, which is why the theological substructure of the New Testament reflects so much of its vocabulary and so many of its insights, quotations, and idioms. Even the writings of Paul suggest that he was more accustomed to the Greek Version (LXX) than to the Hebrew Scriptures, and although he did know Hebrew, he appears to have preferred the LXX when quoting.[28]

---

27. See Emil Schurer, *The History of the Jewish People in the Age of Jesus Christ (175 BC–AD 135)*, vol. 3, Part 1, new English version, revised and edited by Geza Vermes, et al (Edinburgh, Scotland T. & T. Clark, Ltd., 1986), p. 474.

28. See E. Earle Ellis, *Paul's Use of the Old Testament* (Grand Rapids, MI: Wm. E. Eerdmans Publishing Co., 1957), especially pp. 12–16; see also Ellis, "Quotations in the New

Whatever the problems noticed in placing the Hebrew Masoretic Text side-by-side with the Septuagint—or side-by-side with the best current translation of each—the main factor is that the writer of Hebrews viewed and trusted and treasured the LXX as an authoritative document, and, more so, as a Voice text through which God, Christ, and the Holy Spirit are heard speaking. As a document, the LXX reported a past, but the LXX was also a present and vital witness. The writer's statement at 4:12 shows his theology of the Word he read and heard therein, and that theology undergirds the faith stance which made his personal witness so gripping:

> *Indeed, the word of God is living and active, sharper than any two-edged sword, piercing until it divides soul from spirit, joints from marrow; it is able to judge the thoughts and intentions of the heart.*

Influenced always by the Scriptures, the writer steadily appealed to what they offered him: some pregnant line, some significant event, some signal term, and occasionally some personally gripping quote. Now and again he must have been quoting from memory, perhaps at Hebrews 10:37–38, because along with the lines he mentioned from Habakkuk (2:3–4)—again without being verbatim and with some difference in focus—he added a line that appears close to Isaiah 28:16b. Whether he was quoting from memory or from some written source is not clear, but one thing remains certain: the writer was a preacher who lived with the Scriptures, who drank deep from the fountain of truth opened in them, and who lived to share the message they present. Personal faith, depth learning, pastoral passion, and

---

Testament," *International Standard Bible Encyclopedia*, Vol. 4 (Grand Rapids, MI: Wm. B. Eerdmans Publishig Co., 1988, rev. ed.), pp. 18–25.

prophetic insights from the Scriptures are all evident in the letter he wrote to the Hebrews:

> He ate and drank the precious Words—
> His Spirit grew robust—[29]

There was nothing accidental about that preacher's working knowledge of the Septuagint. He studied those Scriptures intensively, examined them thoroughly, trusted them fully, and appropriated them humbly. And this letter of his remains written evidence of the preaching that doubtless followed.

Studying the Scriptures is stern work, and those who avidly do so and humbly receive and appropriate them, are doubly blessed when they find themselves drafted to be a glad and obedient servant of the Word.

Frederick William Robertson (1816–1853) had appropriated Hebrews 4:15–16 in responsible fashion and knew what that central message in Hebrews could mean for his Brighton congregation as he refocused the message of that text in his sermon on "The Sympathy of Christ."[30] His treatment was doctrinal, devotional, and pastoral, with a two-division structure:

I. *The Redeemer's preparation for His priesthood.*
II. *The Redeemer's priestly qualifications:*
    A.   mercifulness, based on his sympathies.
    B.   helpfulness, based on his power to grant aid.

---

29. Emily Dickinson, poem number 1587 in *The Complete Poems of Emily Dickinson*, edited by Thomas H. Johnson (Boston: Little, Brown and Co., 1961), p. 658.

30. Frederick William Robertson, *Sermons Preached at Brighton* (New York: Harper & Brothers, 1947), pp. 88–98.

Robertson is credited with forwarding a new style of outlining through his two-point design. Although he was not the first to use that design, his name became associated with it as his sermons were published and reached a wide audience throughout the English-speaking world. Greatly influenced by Rector Archibald Boyd, with whom for awhile he served at Christchurch in Cheltenham, England, Robertson's sermons were models of compactness and careful workmanship. He lifted the principle of balancing aspects of a text through a two-point arrangement to new heights. James R. Blackwood, a Robertson biographer, has explained that Robertson "adapted this method, developed it, made it characteristically his own, and by his example finally spread it to the ends of the English-speaking world."[31]

John Albert Broadus (1827–1895) also wanted believers to understand the present ministry of the exalted Christ, and he used Hebrews 7:25 in a sermon titled after that verse: "He Ever Liveth to Intercede."[32] "Perhaps we are accustomed to look too exclusively to the Saviour's atoning death,"

---

31. James R. Blackwood, *The Soul of Frederick William Robertson: The Brighton Preacher* (New York: Harper & Brothers, 1947), p. 50. If the question is raised about the importance of Robertson of the nineteenth century as an example, one of the best answers is supplied by O. C. Edwards Jr., who wrote: "While in many ways his age seems as alien to the present as many that are more remote, the situation of the church in the world was so much the same that his example can still be followed with profit" (*A History of Preaching* [Nashville, TN: Abingdon Press, 2004], p. 611). Edwards has further stated that Robertson was one of the first preachers to reinforce for his people the Christian construction of reality as they dealt with belief, practice, and social issues; he helped believers "to face the issues that have been characteristic for mainline Christianity ever since, and that he dealt with them in ways that were effective" (Ibid., p. 609).

32. *Favorite Sermons of John A. Broadus*, edited by Vernon L. Stanfield (New York: Harper & Brothers, 1959), pp. 28–37. On the importance of Broadus for preachers, it is important to note that he was famed as both a biblical scholar (New Testament) and homiletician whose book on preaching (*A Treatise on the Preparation and Delivery of Sermons* [1870]) was a standard work in the field in America across more than a century; generations of seminarians were taught from that book as they studied homiletics.

he acknowledged, "not dwelling as we should upon the idea of his inter-ceding life."[33] The sermon explained and illustrated what the believer can expect and experience because Jesus continues ministering in his exalted role as intercessor. Broadus used a six-point outline:

1. We have his help to conquer temptation.

2. We have an Advocate if we should sin.

3. We have help to attain holiness.

4. We have comfort when in sorrow.

5. We have hope when we die.

6. We have the pledge of a new body like his.

Both Robertson and Broadus understood the central message of Hebrews and wanted their hearers to understand the full ministry of Jesus that is steadily offered and readily available. Both preachers sermonized their text with their concern directed steadily toward the need, interest, and experience of their hearers. Their methods differed, as did their gifts for design, but both had been mastered by the meaning they sought to share.

As for sermon design, this must be said: The design a sermon should have and follow is often dictated by what one hears being spoken in the text to be treated, and by anticipating how those who are to hear it can best receive its message. Frederick William Robertson usually "discerned" a contrast as he studied a text and prepared it for pulpit use, thus his customary two-point outline. Alexander Maclaren (1826–1910) "discerned" three points

33. Ibid., p. 30.

when he examined a text and thought about his Manchester hearers. In an obituary tribute published in *The British Weekly* when Maclaren died in 1910, editor W. Robertson Nicoll wrote:

> Every one knows his method of preaching. His people, as one of his friends said, "were fed with a three-pronged fork." He had an extraordinary gift of analyzing a text. He touched it with a silver hammer, and it immediately broke up into [three] natural and memorable divisions, so comprehensive and so clear that it seemed wonderful that the text should have been handled in any other way. He sought to give truth an edge; he brought everything to a point.[34]

Interestingly, Maclaren never desired to publish his sermons, but after W. Robertson Nicoll strongly suggested that he should do so, his now classic—and highly influential—*Expositions of Holy Scripture* was steadily prepared and released.

Whatever one's sermonic giftedness, two things are to be remembered: the same design pattern will not fit every textual genre with equal success, and most texts can be handled in more than one way. Generally, however, every text demands and deserves its own mode of treatment in keeping with its structure and its mood.

Frederick William Robertson used the exhortation found at Hebrews 4:15–16 to teach and comfort, and John A. Broadus used the doctrinal text at Hebrews 7:25 similarly. William E. Sangster (1900–1960), whose preaching at Westminster Central Hall, London, made him legendary, used Hebrews 13:12–13, with its reference to the place where Jesus died ("outside

---

34. W. Robertson Nicoll, *Princes of the Church* (London: Hodder and Stoughton, Ltd., 1921), pp. 249–50.

the city gate"), to exhort and challenge his hearers about accepting the cost of discipleship—a prime concern in Hebrews. Sangster titled the sermon "Bearing His Reproach."[35] Using a three-fold outline, Sangster advised:

I. *We must accept the reproach of the gospel:*

    A. When ostracized socially

    B. When we lose out on professional advancement because of our faith.

    C. When we are made the butt of jokes

II. *We must not increase the reproach unnecessarily:*

    A. By any eccentricies on our part

    B. By being censorious

    C. By severing fellowship.

III. *We must show an eager willingness to suffer for Christ when we are made to suffer.*

    A. Exult in the suffering—it is His!

All in all, Sangster's sermon was a bracing statement about the cost of discipleship—and the blessedness of "thrusting one's shoulder underneath his cross," the very action to which readers of Hebrews were encouraged to commit themselves (Heb 12:3, 7, 11, 12–13; 13:20–21).

The sharing of guidelines and examples in this chapter has been to assist in developing a responsible pulpit approach to the handling of the Letter to the Hebrews. The homiletic traits of the writer to the Hebrews have been examined for some guidance about the rules that govern the communication process, and his hermeneutic has been assessed for its accent on the resourcefulness of the Scriptures for sermons. Peter T. Forsyth (1848–1921) advised that in an age when the Bible has ceased to be the text book of the people, the preacher must regard it as his or her basic text as we "adjust our preaching to

---

35. See William E. Sangster, "Bearing His Reproach," in *The Twentieth Century Pulpit*, vol. 1, edited by James W. Cox (Nashville, TN: Abingdon Press, 1978), pp. 180–87.

the people's disuse of the Bible."[36] "You are there not simply to speak what people care to hear but also to make them care for what you must speak."[37]

In connection with Forsyth's admonition, it is imperative that the preacher not major on the biographical and illustrative "miniatures" in Hebrews 11 and neglect the letter's grand theme of the cross. Although once universally recognized as the symbol of the Christian faith, the truth once conveyed by that word and image needs to be restated and explained to make possible a wholesome recognition of how salvation happens, and how it must be valued. George A. Buttrick, a master preacher, offered some illuminating counsel about how to do this in his *Jesus Came Preaching,* the last chapter of which treats "The Preaching of the Cross."[38] Buttrick lamented that the cross has become "a theme deplorably strange to modern pulpits but never more imperative." How did the neglect of that theme happen? The impact upon the modern mind of an easy view of sin; an unthinking optimism; an emphasis on externals; an attitude of self-sufficiency based on material wealth and mechanical power; and the bewildering array of theories about the cross. Buttrick centered attention on the life Jesus offered to God and how the holy compassion of his outpoured life gave redemptive virtue to the blood he shed on our behalf. His four suggestions on how to preach about the cross were, and still remain, pertinent:

> 1. Preach the cross as the revelation of God, as the one clue in an often unintelligible world. [Notice the tie-in with the sermon perspective of Arthur Gossip's sermon on Hebrews 2:8–9, "On the Clue to Life's Enigmas."]

---

36. Peter T. Forsyth, *Positive Preaching and Modern Mind: Lyman Beecher Lectures at Yale* (London: Hodder and Stoughton, 1907), p. 36.

37. Ibid., p. 137.

38. George Arthur Buttrick, *Jesus Came Preaching: Christian Preaching in the New Age* (New York: Charles Scribner's Sons, 1951), see pp. 193ff.

2. Preach the cross as the way to life—as the best wisdom for human conduct;

3. Preach the cross as God's power;

4. Preach the cross as salvation from sin and unto life eternal.

Again Buttrick: "Apostolic preaching had but one word—Christ. Apostolic preaching linked to that Word one overmastering adjective: 'Christ crucified.'"[39] They knew it was their assignment to do so.

The writer to the Hebrews understood his given task as he chided some hearers with these words: "We have much to say that is hard to explain, since you have become dull in understanding…You need milk, not solid food." (Heb 5:11, 12b). As an able, concerned, Word-informed preacher, he was ready, using intentional texts with conscious artistry, to meet both diets, intent to motivate and move believers "on towards perfection [maturity]" (6:1).[40] Such is the preacher's task, and the Letter to the Hebrews can assist the preacher in fulfilling that task.

Table of Sermons

The table of sermons that follows is based on the examination of *Twenty Centuries of Great Preaching,* edited by Clyde E. Fant Jr. and William M. Pinson Jr. (Waco, TX: Word Books, 1971), one of the most inclusive encyclopedias of preaching, to ascertain the number of sermons in the set that are based on texts from Hebrews. This multivolume set contains 406 sermons, which represent the pulpit work of ninety-six pulpit masters who spoke effectively to the issues and needs of the church in their day. Only ten among the 406 sermons are based on texts from Hebrews. The

---

39. Ibid., p. 195.
40. On the concept of "intentional texts," see David Buttrick, *Homiletic: Moves and Structures* (Philadelphia: Fortress Press, 1987), pp. 301–3.

Text in Hebrews	Preacher and Sermon Title	Location in Set
2:9	William Booth (1829–1912) "The Atonement of Jesus Christ" [Titus 2:11 with Hebrews 2:9]	V:216–226
6:19	W. E. Sangster (1900–1960) "When Hope Is Dead—Hope On!" [1 Corinthians 13:13 with Hebrews 6:19]	XI:363–368
9:26	James S. Stewart (1896–1990) "The Divine Strategy" [Hebrews 10:4 with Hebrews 9:26]	X:213–216
11:5	George Whitefield (1714–1770) "Walking With God" [Genesis 5:24 with Hebrews 11:5]	III: 146–159
11:5	John Albert Broadus (1827–1895) "And Enoch Walked With God" [Genesis 5:24 with Hebrews 11:5]	V:84–88
11:8	Halford E. Luccock (1885–1960) "The Old-Time Religion" [Exod. 5:1 with Hebrews 11:8]	X:15–18

Text in Hebrews	Preacher and Sermon Title	Location in Set
11:8	Peter Marshall (1902–1949) "Under Sealed Orders" [Genesis 12:1–3 with Hebrews 11:8]	XII:31–42
11:34	Norman Vincent Peale (1898–1993) "New Strength Over Old Weaknesses"	XI:256–262
12:1–2	Ralph W. Sockman (1889–1970) "The Eternal and the Timely" [Hebrews 13:8 with Hebrews 12:1–2]	X:194–200
12:16	Clovis Chappell (1882–1972) "The Sensualist"	IX:217–222
13:8	E. Stanley Jones (1884–1973) "Religion at the Judgment Bar"	IX:323–325
13:20–21	James S. Stewart (1896–1990) "The Power of His Resurrection"	XI:98–202

III. Illustrative Sermons

An Advent Sermon: He Was Like Us

*Therefore he had to become like his brothers and sisters in every
respect,...to make a sacrifice of atonement for the sins of the people.*
—Hebrews 2:17

*Consequently, when Christ came into the world, he said, "Sacrifices
and offerings you have not desired, but a body you have prepared for
me." —Hebrews 10:5*

A Sunday school booklet published some years ago gave some of us
a momentary start. Part of a new approach for teaching three-year-
old children about Jesus, it depicted his disciples dressed in slacks, colorful
sport coats, and with short hair, and Jesus, their leader, dressed in Bermuda
shorts![1] The publishing council of a responsible church body had endorsed
the publication, wanting their children to understand that Jesus was like us.
He was, although the Jesus of history was a Hebrew peasant who did not
dress in the modern garb of the West. But artists have often bypassed
the known facts about him, intent on portraying Jesus more familiarly, to
show his kinship to their own people group. The concern, again, has been
to say that Jesus was like us. He surely was! But he was like us in a more
exemplary way, and, according to our chosen texts, for a most fundamental
reason: The Son of God took on flesh and blood, became an embodied
human, "to make a sacrifice of atonement for the sins of the people."

---

1. See News Section, "Christ Depicted in Modern Dress," *Christianity Today*, November
7, 1960, p. 31.

I

Jesus was born into the world as the incarnate Son of God, and nothing was more obvious in his coming than his human kinship with the rest of us. The many artists who have sought to depict his humanness have had valid reason to do so, and their attempts have been meritorious.

While making pastoral visits I noticed in several homes a reproduction of Warner Sallman's *Head of Christ* adorning one of the walls. The story behind Sallman's rendering is inspirational and quite gripping.

On a certain night in 1924, according to his account, Warner Sallman was groping about in his mind for an art idea out of which he could shape a design for the cover of the religious magazine of his church. As the staff artist, cover designs were his responsibility. The needed design was due by morning and his mind was stubbornly unproductive despite all anxious care.

Kept awake by anxiety over his assignment, Sallman never got to sleep, and at some point close to morning a fresh idea began to fill his mind: a picture of Jesus, complete in every detail, he reported, had formed itself upon the wall of his mind. What startled Sallman was the fact that the features he envisioned for the picture were different from anything he had seen before. He arose from bed, hurried to his attic studio, and swiftly sketched out the inward vision. He met the next-day deadline.[2]

Some years later, through a combination of some unusual circumstances, Sallman's original charcoal drawing of the head of Christ began to gain attention. He re-did the picture in oils, and the full color both added to its attractiveness and aided further sales. Warner Sallman's *Head of Christ* is only an artist's conception of how Jesus looked, but many have been inspired by the features he depicted of a man with Hebrew

---

2. See Harold L. Phillips, editorial, "How It Came About," *The Gospel Trumpet*, July 16, 1961, p. 3.

features, marked by an Oriental tan, and with the bearing of a mature leader-type. No word or description has come to us from the first century about how Jesus actually looked, but like other depictions of its type, Sallman's artistic conception of Jesus reminds us that Jesus was like us and that his humanity was real and thoroughgoing. "He had to become like his brothers and sisters in every respect," the text tells us. The incarnation is in view here: "so that he might…make a sacrifice of atonement for the sins of the people."

II

He became like us "so that he might…make a sacrifice of atonement" on our behalf. The Son of God took on "flesh and blood" on purpose. The "so that" in our first text is crucial, and our second text reminds us that the Son chose our flesh and blood existence to meet our need for atonement: "a body you have prepared for me."

Harold J. Ockenga, an esteemed preacher friend whose admirable pulpit gifts heightened the import of any text he used, described this text once as part of a farewell dialogue in heaven between God the Father and God the Son just before the first Christmas. Having noted how the text quotes Psalm 40:6–8 here and that the words are credited to Christ, Ockenga imagined himself overhearing the Son, on the night before Christmas, thanking his Father for preparing the body with which he was about to enter into the world to carry out his atoning mission.[3]

The *birth* event allowed the Son's embodiment to do what the "scroll of the book" had stipulated as necessary to effect a true and full atonement. Listen again to the passage:

---

3. See Harold John Ockenga, "The Night Before Christmas," in *Great Sermons on the Birth of Christ*, compiled by Wilbur M. Smith (Natick, MA: W. A. Wilde Co, 1963), p. 221ff.

Consequently, when Christ came into the world,
he said [speaking to God the Father],
"Sacrifices and offerings you have not desired,
but a body you have prepared for me;
in burnt offerings and sin offerings
you have taken no pleasure.

Then I said, "See, God, I have come
to do your will, O God."
(in the scroll of the book it is written of me). [10:5–7]

Ockenga's expresssive statement about all this was well warranted: "What a night Christmas Eve was in the spiritual heavens!"[4]

III

The season of Advent is upon us, and the usual trappings that entangle our thoughts and steal our time have little, if anything, to do with what this season really concerns. Advent is the season of expectation, and it is best observed when the reason for the coming of God's Son among us is clearly understood and rightly valued. The coming of Jesus among us was his preparation for service on our behalf. He came among us, as one of us, "to make a sacrifice of atonement for the sins of the people." He came to perform the atoning deed to handle our sins, rid us of them, and save us from our faulty path. The news about the meaning of it all is news about a rescue action, a ransom mission.

---

4. Ibid., p. 221.

Behold, the world's Creator wears
The form and fashion of a slave;

Our very flesh our Maker shares,
His fallen creature, man, to save.
He shrank not from the oxen's stall,
He lay within the manger-bed,
And he whose bounty feedeth all
At Mary's breast himself was fed.[5]

Jesus came among us, made like us, but unlike us, he did no sin; therefore, he can handle our sins if we let him. He came to do God's will. He succeeded in his obedience, so he can help us learn to obey. Jesus stayed in touch with God, and he can put us in right relation to God. He was like us, so that we can become like him. Robert Browning voiced it well in these picturesque lines:

A Face like my face that receives thee;
A Man like to me
Thou shalt love and be loved by, forever:
A Hand like this hand
Shall throw open the gates of new life to thee!
See the Christ stand![6]

IV

There is another detail to Warner Sallman's story about his sleepless night in 1924. After the search ended for an idea to use in preparing that magazine cover, Sallman recalled a conversation held years earlier between himself and the dean of the Bible school he had attended.

---

5. From "A solis ortus cardine," as cited by E. L. Mascall, *The Importance of Being Human* (New York: Columbia University Press, 1958), p. 94.

6. Robert Browning, from "Saul," stanza 18, lines 310ff.

Having heard that young Sallman was a creative artist, the dean had encouraged him to use his gift in Christian service. "We need Christian artists," he had instructed. "And say, sometime I hope you give us your conception of Christ. And I hope it's a manly one. Most of our pictures today are too effeminate." He then added, "We need a picture of that kind of Christ, Sallman, and I hope you do it some day."[7] Sallman confessed that he had thought now and again about the dean's suggestion, but that he had never felt capable of handling such a high task. When he finally handled that task, he felt he had been divinely helped.

We humans can be more than we normally are, and we can do more than we normally do—if we receive divine help. Jesus came to give us that help: he can help us to *be* like him and to *do* the will of God, as he did. He grants that help to all who willingly receive him.

_____

7. See Harold L. Phillips, editorial, "How It Came About," *The Gospel Trumpet*, July 16, 1961, pp. 3–4.

A Lenten Sermon:
The Days of His Flesh

In the days of his flesh, Jesus offered
up prayers and supplications, with loud
cries and tears, to the one who was able
to save him from death, and he was heard
because of his reverent submission. —Hebrews 5:7

Four ministers were at a convention, awaiting the arrival of a noted radio preacher who was scheduled to address an assembly of church leaders. The four talked favorably about his qualities: "He's the best preacher I know," said one. "He's a better pastor than preacher," said another. A third one spoke about him as a friend. The fourth man in the group was older, and ventured this comment: "I think that he is all that you have said. But he is more. If I were going to sum him up in a sentence, I would say that he is intensely human and intensely Christian."[8] That guest preacher stood tall in their view. By calling, gift, or circumstance he was viewed as possessing that something more, that uniqueness by which some persons gain distinction within our ranks. The New Testament tells us about the distinctiveness of Jesus, how he possessed that something more called divinity, and yet he was intensely human. Our text recalls a crucial time when that humanness was under great strain, and how God helped him to live through it. It recalls that awesome night in the Gethsemane garden when Jesus struggled in prayer while facing the final demands of the "days of his flesh."

---

8. The minister being discussed was S. Parkes Cadman. See Fred Hamlin, *S. Parkes Cadman: Pioneer Radio Minister* (New York: Harper & Brothers, 1930), pp. 137–38.

I

It must be said: The days of his flesh were like our days: *they were days of pilgrimage.* Jesus lived and learned as a pilgrim in life, and he shared with other pilgrims what he gained. His discourses and counsel did not emerge from untested thought, The seeds of his contemplation fell and grew up in the soil of human experience. Jesus knew the crises all humans face; he was not spared the common ventures that are inevitable due to being alive. He had to live as we live by watching with faith, a determined spirit, and a careful step. Moving always with his view cast ahead, caught between past and future in a demanding present, the days of his flesh were like our own: a pilgrimage.

II

His days were also *days of peril.* Jesus lived almost constantly under the shadow of death. This was the case since his early childhood.

You will surely recall the report Matthew's gospel gives about the family's narrow escape from the slaughter Herod ordered against innocent infants in an effort to slay the infant Jesus (Matt 2:20). John's gospel reports that across his ministry years, Jesus always had to guard his steps, avoid certain places at certain times, and sometimes shorten his visits here or there because there were those "looking for an opportunity to kill him" (7:1).

Jesus knew what it meant to face peril. Galilee, where he grew to manhood, was a hazardous setting, and all the more because of the Roman soldiers who steadily hounded and harassed the minority populace filled with suspected zealots. From Galilee to Samaria to Judea, peril was a constant fact in his life and ministry.

The perils we face as humans are many, and from more than one source. Peril can arise out of pure circumstance. Peril can result due to unforeseen factors. Peril can result from human opposition, from calculated cruelties, and nothing so threatens as when a human hand is stretched out against us, when the peril is seen as well as felt!

Seven years before Martin Luther King Jr. was assassinated, *Harper's* magazine carried an article by James Baldwin titled, "The Dangerous Road before Martin Luther King."[9] Many of us still remember with sadness what happened only a few years later as that American Moses rounded a dark bend on his pilgrimage. An assassin's bullet ended his days among us. Dr. King had chosen that road, but with peaceful concern to reach the promised land of full freedom, and intent to carry a hounded and harassed people with him.

Dr. King's path had been dangerous all along. Perhaps you recall some of the perils he and his fellow ministers experienced during the desegregation struggle in Montgomery. In his *Stride Toward Freedom,* the book about the Montgomery bus boycott and the opposition faced because of it, the story is replete with threats issued daily against leaders of the protest, and about the letters and telephone calls which kept the sense of peril alive and present.[10] There was one night in 1958 when a bomb was thrown and exploded on the porch of his house. Two years later, he was stabbed while autographing books in a Harlem bookstore. King was within a sneeze of losing his life from that stabbing, because the eight-inch long blade of the letter-opener his attacker used had penetrated to within a fraction of a inch of his aorta, "and a cough, sneeze or twist of the body might have resulted in the puncture of [that] artery," the doctors explained.[11]

---

9. See James Baldwin, "The Dangerous Road Before Martin Luther King," *Harper's Magazine*, February 1961.

10. See Martin Luther King Jr., *Stride Toward Freedom: The Montgomery Story* (New York: Harper & Brothers, 1958), pp. 132ff.

11. See Lawrence D. Reddick, *Crusader without Violence: A Biography of Martin Luther King, Jr.*, (New York: Harper & Brothers, 1959), pp. 229–30.

An assassin did end Dr. King's life in 1968, and America still mourns his loss. He died as a victim of calculated evil. So did John F. Kennedy five years earlier, and so did Robert F. Kennedy, John's brother, shortly after Dr. King was killed. Persons intent to forward public purpose always live under the shadow of death, especially when they speak truth to the powers that be.

Fortunately, the constant sense of peril did not dissuade Dr. King and other reformers we acclaim. To be sure, some persons disquieted by a sense of peril either slowed their action to a cautious pace or succumbed to fear and quit their work. Most of us have lived long enough to know that what we feel and do when trouble comes depends partly on when it comes, partly on what it demands of us, partly on any previous experience we have had with trouble, and partly upon our sense of alternatives and the state of our inner resources. Jesus lived and labored with a determination strengthened by his sense of purpose; his God-assigned task claimed his attention and allegiance, so he never quit his work. He wisely delayed action sometimes when assaulted, but he was too strongly set in heart and will to leave unfinished what he knew God directed him to do.

III

The Gospels report that our Lord's days were also *days of prayer.* Open Luke's account at nearly any spot and you will find Jesus at prayer: He prayed before acting, seeking guidance and strength. He prayed after acting, to give thanks and to be refreshed. For Jesus, prayer was not a singular pious action that excluded other tasks; it was a central experience within which an ordered wholeness of view was gained and by which his will remained centered. Prayer, for Jesus, was always a creative encounter with God.

Our text recalls a particular prayer that Jesus uttered to God out of his pain. Jesus was in the garden of Gethsemane, praying about his approaching death. The experience was so intense that his prayer included "loud cries and tears," meaning his outcries were strenuously uttered with accompanying tears. The text reports that Jesus was asking God to "save him from death." Political pressures and religious zealots had combined against him, and Jesus knew what he would face later that night and across the next day. His spirit was heavy about it all, so he was talking it through with God. Luke (the physician) even reported that the physical agonies Jesus underwent while praying in the Garden included bloody sweating, what is medically known as *hematidrosis* (22:43–44). That olive grove was itself a scene of impending death!

> He wrestled there in agony;
> With drops of sweat of crimson hue
> His brow was wet, as with the dew,
> In tears He knelt, with troubled soul;
> While there he felt death's sorrows roll.[12]

God heard Jesus, the text reports, yet Jesus died the next day! Yes, but with the calmness of spirit that prayer grants and with a self-surrender that matched the demands of death. Actually, the wording of our text should be read as suggesting that due to the physical and spiritual intensity of his experience in the garden, Jesus was praying for God to *save him from dying in the garden,* so that he could die sacrificially on the cross![13] His prayer was heard, that is, answered: It was answered *initially* in that Jesus was saved from dying there in the garden and answered *fully* in the resurrection event, three days after he offered his life on the cross to effect our atonement to God.

> For Thy blest cross which doth for all atone,
> Creation's praises rise before Thy throne.[14]

---

12. Clara M. Brooks, "Thy Will Be Done," Hymn No. 76, *Hymns and Spiritual Songs* (Anderson, IN: Gospel Trumpet Co., n.d.).

13. See Thomas Hewitt, *The Epistle to the Hebrews: An Introduction and Commentary* (Tyndale Bible Commentary) (Grand Rapids, MI: Wm. B. Eerdmans Publishing Co., 1960), pp. 99–101. The argument turns on the meaning of the Greek prepositional phrase *ek, tou thanatou,* "from, out of" death.

14. From "Lift High the Cross," *Worship the Lord: Hymnal of the Church of God* (Anderson, IN: Warner Press, 1989), 69.

IV

The days of his flesh were *days of purpose,* and God crowned that fulfilled purpose when he raised Jesus from death, holding the rank of Savior and Lord.

Jesus lived with a sense of purpose as he pilgrimaged among us, facing perils and communing with God in prayer. He invested his trust in God, which helps us to understand how he managed his pilgrimage so worthily. "Although he was a Son, he learned obedience through what he suffered; and having been made perfect [mature], he became the source of eternal salvation for all who obey him," the rest of the passage tells us (Heb 5:8).

Like us, Jesus had to wrestle with the details of life and the forces of history, but he had decided wisely the lines his life would follow, and he never swerved from what he knew to be God's will for his life. What was initially personal and private in his life has become public through his victorious obedience to God.

Jesus has emerged within history with a redemptive name, and by God's will he manifests a saving and lordly influence that has been granted to no other. We see in him that "something more" that helps to make one's life count. As we ponder his life, we see some of what is possible in our own, and as we open ourselves to his influence, we will find him unfailingly resourceful in the living of our days.

> I have decided to follow Jesus;
> I have decided to follow Jesus;
> I have decided to follow Jesus;
> No turning back,
>
> No turning back.
> (Folk melody from India)

A Stewardship Sermon:
On Being Responsible

By faith Moses, when he was grown up, refused to be called a son of Pharaoh's daughter, choosing rather to share ill-treatment with the people of God than to enjoy the fleeting pleasures of sin. He considered abuse suffered for the Christ to be greater wealth than the treasures of Egypt, for he was looking ahead to the reward.— Hebrews 11:24–26

At times in our lives we must make a personal decision that we know will affect us totally and even determine the course of our future. Those are times when an independent and informed choice is demanded, and we must be personally responsible and act. Hebrews 11 describes how Moses faced such a time in his life. His exact age is not given, but the text reports he had grown up. His age, his circumstances, and his awareness had converged to make a decisive choice necessary concerning his future. It was a crucial time. He knew that he would have to go in one direction or another. So, crowded by circumstance, he ponders his options; compelled by conviction, he acts responsibly and decides his future.

The account is highly abbreviated. It has the "laconic terseness" that novelist Thomas Mann used to lament when reading biblical stories. Mann wished he could know each biblical story "as life first told it,"[15] and so do we. However, despite the abbreviation of the record, our text commends the choice Moses made and it reports the grand outcome. Although lacon-

---

15. See Thomas Mann, *Joseph in Egypt*, vol. 11 (New York: Alfred A. Knopf. 1938), especially pp. 370–71. Trans. from the German by H. T. Lowe-Porter.

ically terse, the Hebrews 11 account offers us needed wisdom about how to be responsible before God.

I

Having grown up, Moses *acted responsibly by embracing the full facts about himself.* Armed with the knowledge that he was a Hebrew, Moses dropped that designation under which he had lived since a child, son of Pharaoh's daughter.

Something deep within Moses stirred him to do this. Why else would he disavow such privilege and power? Moses had been granted an elevated status, the result of having been claimed for life by Pharaoh's daughter, a kind benefactress. As her adopted son, Moses had the benefits of Egyptian culture and learning—even the possibility of becoming a pharaoh. Moses must have known that Egypt had been ruled and governed by non-Egyptian pharaohs and advisors before, so he must have been mightily stirred from within when, having now grown up, he willfully refused to claim that granted heritage any longer.

My wife Gwendolyn and I were serving under appointment in Jamaica in 1966 when two royal figures visited that nation. One of them was Her Royal Highness Queen Elizabeth of England. The visit of the queen was marked by quiet dignity during the public gathering and a state reception. But one month later, Emperor Haile Selassie I, a black, diminuitive, elderly king from Ethiopia, visited Jamaica. His visit became an event of tremendous public drama. I shall never forget the resounding shout from the black populace when he emerged from his airplane. A jubilant mass of black men, two thousand strong, released that pride-filled shout honoring the black head of one of the most ancient empires in history and someone with whom they felt a ready identity. It was a deafening roar of welcome, accompanied by a virtual forest of palm leaves being waved in his honor. It was a welcome fit for a king.

People do special things for royalty, and a responsible royalty can do significant things for common people. Something special, working deep within Moses, persuaded him to forego the possibility of possessing and using the powers of a king. That stirring surely included a deep appreciation of his Hebrew heritage. Continuing to be regarded as son of Pharaoh's daughter would not have honored the truth Moses knew about himself. He chose to embrace and declare the full facts about himself, mindful of the cost involved in doing so.

Nursed by his own mother, as we know from the account in Exodus, Moses was doubtless informed and influenced by her. Thus he knew his Hebrew facts, as we might term it. Had learning Hebrew distinctives made Moses abhor the divinity myths honoring the pharaonic order? Had the brutal slavery system over which Pharaoh had full command repulsed Moses' sense of justice and order? Did he feel a need to part company with any style of life that allowed and fed upon the misuse of power?

Whatever his reasons, the text tells us that Moses refused to live any longer as son of Pharaoh's daughter. Perhaps he had met some criticisms and slander from those at court who also knew that he was a Hebrew. Any Egyptian priests who knew this would certainly try to prevent his rise to power, even though he was protected as son of Pharaoh's daughter. The ancient historian Josephus preserved a legend about this: Pharaoh's daughter brought the infant Moses to court one day, and Pharaoh took the boy and held him affectionately to his breast. To please his daughter, Pharaoh took his diadem and placed it on the child's head. When the child playfully knocked the crown off and it fell to the ground, the watching priests interpreted this as an omen of ill against the throne of Egypt.[16] Legends aside, we do know that Moses thoughtfully set aside his title of adopted son and thus closed the door to an imperial life that may have

---

16. See Flavius Josephus, *Antiquities of the Jews*, Book II, Ch.IX, par. 7.

Illustrative Sermons   **171**

been planned by his benefactress. He felt in his heart what his life must affirm and reject. His eyes set, his energies focused, Moses took his stand and honored his convictions.

II

The text tells us that *this responsible action of Moses was decided and accomplished "by faith."* Moses took a calculated risk. He projected his future on the basis of a sensed meaning, persuaded by a moment of truth.

Despite the risks, Moses acted responsibly because he let himself be persuaded by the truth. Søren Kierkegaard wisely declared that "the truth is a snare: you cannot have it without being caught. You cannot have the truth in such a way that you catch it, but only in such a way that it catches you."[17] Moses could not remain in the old life, comfortably settled there, once the truth about himself and his true people seized his heart. Informed by the truth, Moses let himself be influenced by it. Instead of feeling undone, he felt undergirded, ready to risk his future, ready to be responsible.

III

Responsible for what? The shape of his future! Responsible to whom? God! The God whose actions had provided the meanings Moses sensed as imperative for his life.

No word is more central for self-understanding and fulfillment than this one: *responsibility*. We were envisioned and created to be responsible persons, who are fully aware of our options but act in a way that is accountable to the truth. Moses did this. By following the course truth laid out before him, there was an inevitable connection between his future and the Christ God promised to send. According to the writer of Hebrews,

---

17. See Søren Kierkegaard, *The Last Years*, edited and translated by Ronald Gregor Smith (New York: Harper & Row, Publishers, 1965), p. 133.

"He considered abuse suffered for the Christ to be greater wealth than the treasures of Egypt, for he was looking ahead to the reward."

The person of faith wisely looks ahead because faith grants an anticipating and connecting link with the future. If Moses had nostalgically looked back, he might have lamented his losses. If he had selfishly looked around, he might have stooped and staggered under the weight of abuse he received. His decision to forego the patronage of Pharaoh's daughter meant that he would no longer have granted royal status and guaranteed imperial protection. He would have to leave Egypt or share in the ill-treatment suffered by the Hebrews, his own people. He had made his decision, and despite the cost, there was no going back.

Beeson Divinity School Chapel
January 16, 2002

All Saints' Sermon:
Stay in the Race!

Therefore, since we are surrounded by so great a cloud of witnesses, let us also lay aside every weight and the sin that clings so closely, and let us run with perseverance the race that is set before us, looking to Jesus the pioneer and perfecter of our faith, who for the sake of the joy that was set before him endured the cross, disregarding its shame, and has taken his seat at the right hand of the throne of God. —Hebrews 12:1–2

I

Every four years, as the time for the International Olympic Games approaches and we hear news reports of the athletes who will compete in the games, I think of how they must psych their minds, train their bodies, and set their hopes in preparation to be winners. I think about former Olympic winners, some of whom broke old records and set new standards by their skill. I think about the vow that hopeful athletes of ancient times sometimes made to be victorious, and how life-size statues of the winners were sometimes prepared and displayed in the winners' home cities.[18] Some of those statues can be seen in our museums, the athlete's physical development vividly captured in stone by a sculptor's skills.

But I think about something far more important than gold or bronze medals to be gained. When the time for the Olympic Games approaches,

18. See E. Nornan Gardiner, *Athletes of the Ancient World* (Oxford, England: Clarendon Press, 1955), p. 58.

I also think about the scene and summons found in Hebrews 12, a text that never fails to stir my spirit to be a winning Christian in the great race of life.

The *scene* is of an athletic event in process, with a great course laid out on which runners are competing before a vast assemblage of spectators. The *summons* is for Christian believers to view themselves as athletes on the race course of life, the successful handling of which demands due preparation, a tested readiness to undergo strain, and a will trained for endurance. Readiness to become a winning athlete involves this, and so does a successful Christian life.

II

Notice that the text addresses us as athletes and, in the sense I have described, we are. The summons of Hebrews 12 is acute, abrupt, deliberate, pointed, and necessary, because we believers sometimes fail to be as serious in our Christian concerns as athletes who are eager to win competitions. The lack of seriousness shows itself most surely in spiritual unreadiness to handle life's demands. The text mentions "weights" and "clinging sins" as evidences of spiritual unreadiness and strongly urges us to be rid of them.

Athletic readiness has always involved an apt physical development, a well-muscled form, with no flabbiness of flesh. There is in one of the writings of Xenophon the story about Socrates chiding his young colleague Epigenes, who was in poor physical condition. Socrates urged the young man to give himself with seriousness to athletics to build himself physically. Epigenes replied, "I am not an athlete," meaning perhaps that he had no ambition to have a body bulging with muscles like the professionals. But Socrates would not be put off. The young man's body was in poor health; it lacked strength, zest, and beauty. Socrates asked him what benefit he could be to the state in that condition if crisis developed and war came?

He added that only the fit could save themselves. Socrates went on to explain that fitness comes by labor and exacts ongoing care.[19]

Christian victories follow spiritual fitness and are the consequence of our readiness to endure the stress and strain of spiritual adversity. Spiritual fitness does not come of its own accord; it must be gained, and the text tells us how: "Lay aside every weight and the sin that clings so closely, and… run with perseverance…, looking unto Jesus." Every earnest believer will want to understand the demands of the course and remove all personal obstacles that hinder. Whatever burdens our personal intent, whatever might hamper our running wholeheartedly for God, must be laid aside. It should be laid aside willingly, on purpose, and immediately.

As for "the sin that clings so closely," all of us have known some personal and inward problems that can be like a trailing garment that entangles our feet, as it were, and trips us. Problems such as selfish, stubborn, sinful attitudes (nothing can cling closer or trip us faster than an attitude) or mixed motives. Serious discipleship requires us to sift our motives, unravel every twisted concern, and center our intent on God.

A look back at our sinful past will teach each of us about any close clinging sin we have known. Surely you can remember some wrong to which you were personally drawn before God's grace claimed your life. You can also remember certain weak spots, vulnerable places in your life where evil found a somewhat easier entrance into your thoughts and behavior. All of us can remember where we had obvious problems with ourselves before God graciously provided a delivering solution. Our repentance and initial resolve gave God freedom to forgive us and help us where we needed that deliverance. But we must remain watchful, for where we failed before a new spiritual attack can seem hardest to handle. The summons in the text is clear, and its counsel is unmistakable: "Lay aside every weight and the sin

---

19. Xenophon, *Memorabilia and Oeconomicus* (Loeb Classical Library), English Trans. by E. C. Marchant (Cambridge, MA: Harvard University Press, 1953), see pp. 249–53.

that clings so closely." Some problems that subdued us before can subdue us again, unless we take heed and deepen our resolve to stay in the race.

Two of my favorite spirituals from our black American musical heritage are about resolve, about the will to live for God, and honoring one's conviction to the very last struggle in life. Some of you will recognize this portion from one of them:

> Until I reach my home,
> Until I reach my home,
> I never intend to give the journey over,
> Until I reach my home.

Here are lines from the other one:

> Done made my vow to the Lord
> And I never will turn back.
> I will go, I shall go,
> To see what the end will be.[20]

Notice the emphasis on the "vow," with the Lord as its receiving witness. The song says the believer has fully accepted the weight of keeping that vow and fully intends to honor it. A struggle with sin and self has taken place, a decision has been made, and sinful ways have been abandoned, replaced with a firm resolve to live a new life and reach a worthy goal at the end. The end of the process is so important that every ounce of one's strength of resolve and endurance will be devoted to reaching it. That is how athletes stay in the race and gain the desired prize. It is also how serious believers deport themselves in the Christian race.

---

20. On these spirituals, see John Lovell Jr., *Black Song: The Forge and the Flame* (New York: Paragon House Publishers, 1972),. especially pp. 322–23, 379.

III

Having listened afresh to the summons voiced in Hebrews 12, let us look more closely now at the stadium scene the text depicts. As we know, an athletic event is underway, reminiscent of the Olympiad celebrated in the Mediterranean world since the beginning games in 776 BC at Olympia in Greece. Those early Olympics involved Hellenic athletes from near and far, plus multitudes of supporters and spectators who filled the seats of the stadium. The stadium also had a special section with seats reserved for veteran winners from previous contests. Those veterans would sit proudly in their seats of honor, and their presence inspired the athletes competing down on the track. Those veteran winners would sit there watching, concerned, prompting, sometimes applauding—each one a figure and symbol of achievement, a living proof of successful endeavor.

Confident that his readers knew about such matters, the writer of the text draws upon the imagery of a crowded stadium during the Olympics as he seeks to encourage some trouble-weary believers. He urges them to understand themselves as engaged contestants on the great track of life, athletes being watched, prompted, and cheered on by the "great crowd of witnesses" whose faith struggles he had reviewed in chapter 11. "Here you are," he said with pastoral concern, "and there they are!" he suggestively pictured. He seemed to be shouting: "Prophets, priests, and kings are watching you! Warriors, pioneers, fathers and holy women are pulling for you!" The bright-robed witnesses of faith were so numerous as to appear like a great cloud covering the reserved seats in the stadium, each one a hero or heroine of faith. Each one is a responsible, sensitive winner. Each one is a grand soul and achiever, who illustrates by example the awesome strength of faith, the tenacity of perseverance, and the grand dignity of spiritual success, indisputable proof that spiritual preparation and dogged endurance will be rewarded!

Mind you, the text does not minimize the struggle involved in being a believer; in fact, the text underscores that struggle. It tells us plainly that strain and agony are part of the Christian life. The text faces the facts, and it helps us to face those facts by seeing faces which encourage us to endure them. Living as a Christian is no picnic; it is a demanding contest in which we must struggle against evil. The stadium scene in the text, with its pictured host of previous winners, encourages us to expect victory and honor if we answer its summons and stay in the race.

IV

The drama in the text was vividly heightened for me one afternoon many years ago during a very stressful time in my ministry, a time when my spirit needed a lift. I was standing in the well-decorated sanctuary of the St. Peter and St. Paul Russian Orthodox Church building in my home city of Detroit. That church had hosted the monthly meeting of our City Pastors' Union that day, and after the meeting I decided to linger about and study the decorative painted scenes filling the sanctuary walls and ceiling. These had captured my interest as our meeting was in progress. The pastor welcomed my questions. He explained that the paintings on the sanctuary walls and ceiling were the work of a refugee artist, who had worked across seven years to complete the almost lifelike depictions of faith heroes I stood admiring. I remained a while longer after Pastor Lillikovich left the sanctuary, my mind and heart feasting on the meaning and impact of it all. It all made me think about our text, and there deepened in me an understanding of the scene it depicts. I soon felt my heart being "strangely warmed." My thought had moved beyond those painted depictions of apostles and noted Christians from past eras to remember some grand Christian believers, all deceased, whom I myself had known, all of them stalwart saints. Standing there that afternoon, I experienced a high moment of meaning that still blesses my life: Faces of those departed saints seemed to appear to me, with eyes focused in my direction, saying, "Endure the agony! You can yet win! Stay in the race!" I felt strengthened. I felt encouraged. I felt readied for whatever would be next. Strong emotion fills me now as I report this, and I must confess that it seems almost a sacrilege to speak about it.

In 1981, three years before he died, Dr. Benjamin E. Mays published a second book of autobiographical reminiscences. Many of its pages repeated selected narratives given before in his magisterial autobiography, *Born to Rebel;* but in the second book, Mays added details and offered tribute to many persons in his life who had, in his words, "driven him on" by their encouragement and help. Dr. Mays took the time to name those persons because, as he stated, they "inspired me to do things that I never thought I could accomplish."[21]

There are such persons in our world, and some now beyond our world, whose example and experiences inspire us and drive us on. That is why our text pictures for us that "great cloud of witnesses."

V

Like some of you, I have friends in other church bodies whose liturgy includes a duty to commemorate the righteous dead in prayers and praise, especially on All Saints Day. One facet of that concern is to recognize the church as a beloved community of memory as well as hope. Our church tradition may not offer prayers for the dead, but we are wise to remember the dead. We are wiser still if, from time to time, we express our thanks to God for them. Though dead, they still bless us by their remembered walk and worthy work. Our passage in Hebrews 12 reflects this kind of regard for the righteous dead. Our writer views them as "a cloud of witnesses"

---

21. Benjamin E. Mays, *Lord, The People Have Driven Me On* (New York and Atlanta: Vantage Press, 1981), p. 4.

because they were in fact examples of grand achievements through faith, prime examples of what a tested faith means and can produce.

But our writer does not advise us to fix our gaze or set our faith on any of them. He directs us to "look to Jesus, the pioneer and perfecter of our faith."

Yes, there is a gathered throng sitting in the Upper Tier of life. All of those in the throng were good and godly persons through their faith. We each knew some of them. Could we but scan the galleries, penetrating the distance between here and There, we would surely catch sight of a departed friend, a beloved family member, a fellow believer whom we knew well— perhaps a pastor, minister, or sainted spiritual advisor who helped us with needed counsel and a trusted care. Could we but see them, their faces no longer hidden from us by the separating mist of death, we would surely see them watching us, showing eagerness for us, pulling for us. If we could not only look but also listen, we would hear them cheering for us.

Holding the center seat among that gathered throng, however, is another figure. The writer distinguishes him as Jesus, our Savior, and he tells us to fasten our eyes on him because Jesus outshines and outranks all others. He is the One who endured the cross and managed its shame redemptively, thus providing for our salvation. No ordeal we experience can match his; no stress we undergo can be as horrid as his; no struggle we face can be more shameful or demanding than his. Look to Jesus! His victory was so exemplary and effective that it remains not only our inspiration but a source of strength.

Look to Jesus! Can you not see him? Concentrate your gaze in faith! Look! Look to Jesus! He is the One with his hand upon his breast, his heart heaving as he watches us run the course. He knows where we are. He understands the strain we feel, and he is sympathetic as we struggle in the race. Look to Jesus! He wants us to succeed and he steadily prays to

God for us. What greater consolation can we find than this? What greater incentive do we need than this?

Keep looking to Jesus! Be determined! Gather strength from him, and stay in the race!

A Commitment Sermon:
Our Noblest Pursuit

Pursue peace with everyone, and the holiness without which no one will see the Lord.—Hebrews 12:14

Those who are familiar with the camp-meeting scenes of yesteryear will surely recall, as I do, some of the painted signs and oil-cloth banners that adorned the historic tabernacles across the land. One banner I saw had a large eye painted on it; underneath that eye were the words, "The Lord has His eye on you!" That sign made some viewers feel secure and made others shudder. I remember as well a large banner over the pulpit area of one tabernacle that read: "Holiness unto the Lord." That banner kept believers serious. My text is a written banner that prods us to pursue the noblest end of life: the preparation of ourselves to see the Lord of our faith. The writer's directive is forcefully put, and its importance is clearly stated: "Without [holiness] no one will see the Lord."

What is this "holiness" that we are directed to pursue, and how does one pursue it?

I

Holiness is a key teaching in both Testaments concerning God. *Holiness* is a word that describes God's character. It also describes what happens to humans, places, and things when God touches and controls them. In referring to God as "the Holy One," Scripture tells us that God differs in nature from what is ordinary, common, and sinful.

The holiness of God is seen in the person of Jesus, God's Son. In his character and behavior, Jesus manifested God's purity, God's approval, and God's will. Accordingly, this letter to the Hebrews declares that Jesus is "holy, blameless, and undefiled" (7:26).

Jesus is uniquely related to God the Father. Hebrews tells us that "he is the reflection of God's glory and the exact imprint of God's very being" (1:3). We cannot explain such a truth with precision, but we can benefit from the relationship Jesus holds with God by accepting the effects it can produce in and for all who accept and follow him. John's Gospel reports that "all who received him, who believed in his name, he [Jesus] gave power to become children of God" (11:2). Believing on Jesus relates us to God; it grants us access to family status, the granted privilege to belong to, and address God as our Father too. Granted that benefit, we are expected to honor and take on the character of the Father. The holiness we are to pursue, then, is *the likeness of God as seen in Jesus.*

II

We take on the likeness of God by taking Jesus seriously and following him obediently. Following Jesus demands separating ourselves from all known sin; it requires full respect for God's known will and a hunger for an ever-closer walk with Jesus. Only so can godliness be progressively realized in our lives.

Some time ago, I saw and conversed with someone who had known me since my early boyhood and was a close friend of my father. It had been years since we had seen each other. As we chatted about my father, who had died, the elderly friend said: "My, James! You sure do remind me of your father. You are looking more and more like him!" I appreciated that comment and thanked that friend, proud that something about me made him pay tribute to my sainted father. My father was one of my models, and I rejoice that some of his features are stamped in my looks and that aspects of his life have distinctly marked mine. Loving my father as I did, I confess that I pursued being like him in spirit.

Likewise, the pursuit of holiness requires a love for God, time with God, and a deep concern to take on his likeness. When there is a genuine dedication to God's known will; when the self has been surrendered in unreserved fullness to the lordship of Jesus, the result is a progressively qualitative life that reflects God's presence and character.

III

It must be said, then, that the pursuit of holiness must be *individual.* We must each begin and sustain this pursuit personally, and that pursuit must involve and include the total self.

Further, the results of pursuing holiness are *identifiable.* Godly character traits result within us as God's Spirit nurtures us. The apostle Paul identified those character traits as "fruit of the Spirit," and he enumerated them as "love, joy, peace, patience, kindness, generosity, faithfulness, gentleness, and self-control" (Gal 5:22–23).

This experienced holiness is *intelligible.* Living to please God and to exemplify his character makes sense! It always makes sense to live right, and it is foolish, nonsense, to live otherwise. The ancient Hebrews were instructed, "You must follow exactly the path that the LORD your God has commanded you, so that you may live, and that it may go well with you" (Deut 5:23). It always makes sense to do that which is on the side of life rather than death, that which makes things go well rather than go wrong. The pursuit of holiness means accepting certain limitations and observing certain boundaries as we live, but these are limitations and boundaries in the interest of life at its best, so that all of our powers and potential are wisely and intentionally directed and never misdirected or misused. The apostle Peter voiced it like this to the church in his generation: "Discipline yourselves;…Like obedient children, do not be conformed to the desires that you formerly had in ignorance. Instead, as he who called you is holy, be holy yourselves in all your conduct; for it is written, 'You shall be holy, for I am holy'" (1 Pet 1:13b, 14–16).

The life that exemplifies holiness is not only identifiable and intelligible, it is also *instrumental.* Holy living readies us to fulfill the work of divine love as we make our way in this broken and needy world.

Works of love do not happen of themselves; they result from motivated, caring hearts! Works of love issue from hearts touched and ordered by the love of God. The persons initially addressed by the writer of Hebrews needed to be reminded to stay related and responsive to each other. They were being persecuted as Christians, and the pressures they felt had influenced some to withdraw from the fellowship. Some, wanting to escape abuse, were tempted to renounce their faith. It was a time of trouble, tension, questioning, fear, and strained feelings, a time when even closer relations were needed for encouragement and stability. So the writer urged them, "Pursue peace with everyone." Then, building on the same verb, he instructed them to pursue holiness, knowing that harmony between human beings demands more than what is only human. According to Jesus, peacemaking and peace-keeping are godlike: "Blessed are the peacemakers," Jesus said, "for they will be called children of God" (Matt 5:9). Perhaps mindful of this, the writer warned his readers against allowing any "bitterness to spring up and cause trouble, and through it many be defiled" (v 15). Pursuing holiness could ensure a climate of peace in the church and guard them all against failing.

IV

Pursue holiness! God has placed his likeness before us in Jesus, and that likeness is available to us by following Jesus. Following Jesus intently will cleanse, clarify, and discipline our selfhood as we develop in his Image.

Pursue holiness, and the pursuit will be progressively rewarded! After a long struggle with himself, while roaming around with a God-hungry heart, John Wesley discovered this. He afterward declared: "I am now assured that these things are so: I experience them in my own breast. What Christianity (considered as a doctrine) promised is accomplished in my soul... It is holiness and happiness, the image of God impressed on a created spirit, a fountain of peace and love springing up into everlasting life."[22] No wonder, then, that Wesley was so zealous and diligent as he worked so steadily "to reform the [English] nation, particularly the Church, and to spread Scriptural holiness over the land."[23]

Francis Asbury, a contemporary and disciple of Wesley, bore the same testimony. At thirty-one years of age, he confessed, "All my desire is for the Lord, and more of his divine nature impressed on my soul. I long to be lost and swallowed up in God."[24]

Set your heart on God! Follow Jesus Christ! Be done with sin! Pursue holiness, and your quest will be rewarded as well, here in this life and hereafter in the glorious Presence of God!

---

22. See John Wesley's letter to Dr. Conyers Middleton, dated January 4, 1749, in *The Letters of the Rev. John Wesley*, edited by John Telford (London: Epworth Press, 1931), vol. 2, p. 383.
23. See *The Works of the Rev. John Wesley, A.M.*, 3rd ed, edited by Thomas Jackson, vol. 8, p. 299.
24. See *The Journal of Francis Asbury* (London: Epworth Press, 1958), vol. 1, p. 178. The entry is dated Feb. 12, 1776.

A Communion Sermon:
Remember Where You Stand

You have not come to something that can be touched, a blazing fire, and darkness, and gloom, and a tempest, and the sound of a trumpet, and a voice whose words made the hearers beg that not another word be spoken to them. (For they could not endure the order that was given, "If even an animal touches the mountain, it shall be stoned to death." Indeed, so terrifying was the sight that Moses said, "I tremble with fear.") But you have come to Mount Zion and to the city of the living God, the heavenly Jerusalem, and to innumerable angels in festal gathering, and to the assembly of the firstborn who are enrolled in heaven, and to God the judge of all, and to the spirits of the righteous made perfect, and to Jesus, the mediator of a new covenant, and to the sprinkled blood that speaks a better word than the blood of Abel.

See that you do not refuse the one who is speaking; for if they did not escape when they refused the one who warned them on earth, how much less will we escape if we reject the one who warns from heaven! At that time his voice shook the earth; but now he has promised, "Yet once more I will shake not only the earth but also the heaven." This phrase, "Yet once more," indicates the removal of what is shaken—that is, created things—so that what cannot be shaken may remain. Therefore, since we are receiving a kingdom that cannot be shaken, let us give thanks, by which we offer to God an acceptable worship with reverence and awe; for indeed our God is a consuming fire. —Hebrews 12:18–29

I

An awesome fire once blazed on Mount Sinai, manifesting the divine presence to Moses and the newly liberated Hebrew people who had gathered there to receive instructions on how to conduct themselves as his chosen people. Devout Jews still speak about that mountain and what happened there, and they do so with trembling tongues. Exodus 19 tells us why. Those who witnessed the scene, who experienced the theophany and its accompanying features, found themselves filled with terror. A "thick cloud" was God's robe, as it were, while pealing thunder quieted everyone in preparation for the voice of the divine. The cloud, the thunder, the tempestuous winds, the surging smoke that covered the frowning ridges of rock, and the intermittent flashes of awesome fire—all these made the place where the people were standing an arena of terror. The people felt confronted and endangered by God. And when they heard the voice of the Lord (which they had not expected, and for which they found themselves unprepared), the startled throng cried out to be spared. They pleaded "that not another word be spoken [so directly] to them" (12:19). That mount of visitation was a privileged but perilous place.

Our passage from Hebrews 12 recalls all this, and the writer uses it as background for his comments about the present age of blessing and grace since the coming of Jesus. The writer was telling the believers of his day, and us, about the privileged place that grace has allowed believers to experience with respect to God. The text is the writer's word to all believers to remember where we stand.

II

All we who have accepted Jesus as Savior *stand in a new history.* Every believer benefits from the new covenant with God that is now in effect.

Those who received the first covenant stood in a place of awesome command, as the textual passage reminds us. Those gathered at the base of that mountain filled with fire trembled under felt threat. The cloud, the darkness, the winds and fire were a boundary line, an evident barrier that they saw and felt. These were tokens of the divine presence, yes, but they were a sickening judgment as well. God was speaking, yes, but the experience felt more like confrontation than communion. At times, being in the presence of God does not give humans a sense of reassurance! Those are the times when privilege and peril seem strangely intertwined, and peril is felt more acutely than the privilege.

Life under the Decalogue was a mixed blessing. God therefore promised that a new and better arrangement would supersede it, and our text tells us that we now stand within that promised new arrangement. Our time and place in grace is far better than that of the ancient Hebrews who trembled in fear before "a blazing fire, and darkness, and gloom, and a tempest…and a voice whose words made the hearers beg that not another word be spoken to them" (12:18–19).

All of us who have placed faith in Jesus are involved in a new history because of the new covenant God has put into effect through his deed of death on our behalf. This truth is stated and restated throughout the New Testament, but here in Hebrews it is given the most fully articulated emphasis. Again and again, this letter reminds us of the old covenant, the change that God promised, the new covenant arrangement and how it came into effect. Again and again the writer names and exalts Jesus and tells what has happened in history because of him and what happens in a believer's life because of him. Everyone who believes on Jesus as

Savior enters a new history because of Jesus, a new history shaped by him. Everyone who truly believes on him stands in a place of many fulfilled promises, with more fulfilment yet to come. As for now, the promised new covenant is in effect: "I will put my laws in their hearts, and I will write them on their minds" (10:16), and our previous sins and misdeeds are remembered against us no more! This is the new history into which we have entered as believers. This is the grand place where we now stand, and we must gratefully remember and regard it.

III

All who have accepted Jesus as Lord now *stand in a beautiful and beneficial new community.*

Those who submitted to the Law given at Mount Sinai became a congregated chosen people, and yet each person felt appallingly individual as the terror of the scene struck them; each listening spectator felt under judgment because of the superior voice that was speaking. There was no immediate sense of community but a feeling of calamity instead, with each one conscious mainly of personal sin and personal plight because of that sin. This indeed is what made the old covenant such a problem: It made each Hebrew acutely aware of his or her sins and unworthiness!

But Jesus has come among us, claiming believers by his "sprinkled blood that speaks a better [more gracious] word than the blood of [others]" (12:24). Jesus not only claims those who believe, readily and radically cleansing each one by his blood, he also puts believers in relation with each other in a truly beloved community. We who believe are now citizens of "the city of the living God, the heavenly Jerusalem," these being two descriptive terms for the church God has brought together around his Son.

In remembering that we stand in such a community, we will honor the meanings by which the church lives and we will increasingly value the grand fellowship that belonging allows and encourages. The writer was thinking about the purpose of the church and about what belonging means when he cautioned: "See to it that no one fails to obtain the grace of God; that no root of bitterness springs up and causes trouble, and through it many become defiled" (12:15). He was reminding them, and us all, about the beauty and benefits of the new community into which all who believe have been admitted. He wanted each and all to give and receive as full family members, benefitting each other.

A British pastor told of a soldier who attended a worship service at his church during World War II. Observing the man's fighting gear hanging on his tired shoulders, and seeing that it was heavy, the pastor asked how far he could carry such a load. The soldier thought for a minute and replied that he could carry it for about twelve miles. After a slight but thoughtful pause, the soldier added that he could carry his load even farther, perhaps fifteen miles or more, if accompanied by an active band.[25] Yes, the right kind of group does help us accomplish more than we could without their presence and encouragement. A godly and loving church is such a group.

IV

If we are alert believers, we *stand in anticipation that God will bring human history to an intended climax.* We are promised that the conflicts, convulsions, calamities, and contradictions of human history will not continue forever. The textual passage assures us that there will be "the removal of what is shaken—that is, created things—so that what cannot be shaken may remain" (12:27). God will supervise the shaking, God will manage the disruptions, and God will order the settling effects of it all. There is something more to come than we have seen, something that is better, something that is not temporal and ephemeral but permanent, something that will not pass away. That will be the last of all changes.

---

25. See George J. Jeffrey, *This Grace Wherein We Stand* (New York: Charles Scribner's Sons, 1949), pp.29–30.

Preaching from Hebrews

We who trust in Jesus can therefore stand our ground, living by an assured hope. History will be consummated, and we will have an unending future with our Lord: "Therefore," the writer exhorts, " since we are receiving a kingdom that cannot be shaken, let us give thanks, by which we offer to God an acceptable worship with reverence and awe" (12:28).

There is more to come than what we have seen and known. Our present store of experiences through the new covenant is only a foretaste. Meanwhile, however, we must not seek to escape history, lazily waiting for what God will do at the end; we must not postpone essential action or resign from common contacts in life or spend our time wishing. No, we give ourselves to God in worship and steadily work at sharing our faith, giving a steady witness in the world.

V

Are you a believer? If so, then remember where you stand! Jesus has given us a new history, placed us in a new family, and guides us by a new hope. Our lives do not revolve around a place, but they center in a person: Jesus Christ.

We who are believers have not come to a mountain that can be touched, we have come to a Mediator who wants us to relate to him in full faith and faithfulness, and relate to each other in a faithful love. We have not come to a place of terror but into a community founded upon tremendous truths. We "have come to Mount Zion and to the city of the living God, the heavenly Jerusalem, and to innumerable angels in festal gathering, and to the assembly of the first-born who are enrolled in heaven, and to God who is judge of all, and to the spirits of the righteous made perfect, and to Jesus, the mediator of a new covenant ...."

This is where every true believer stands. And we who believe must live by what we understand about the importance of it all. That understanding should show itself in a steady openness to all that God has spoken to us about life and living, an openness inspired by gratitude for grace. That understanding should show itself in our worship, helping us "offer to God an acceptable worship with reverence and awe" (12:28). That understanding should also show itself in our daily work. Thus the writer's prayer that "the God of peace, who brought back from the dead our Lord Jesus, the great shepherd of the sheep, [will] by the blood of the eternal covenant, make [us] complete in everything good so that [we] may do his will, working among [us] that which is pleasing in his sight, through Jesus Christ, to whom be glory forever and ever" (13:20–21).

As a boy, I went with my parents on many occasions to visit friends of the family. In the course of these visits, we attended worship services here and there. After arriving, my Father and Mother always cautioned me to remember where we were and that they expected me to act properly in keeping with where we were. I knew the family rules, I knew the protocol that was to be observed because of who we were and where we were.

During his first year as president of the United States, John F. Kennedy sometimes forgot the protocol surrounding that high office. One day he stepped back in gentility and held a door open for Mrs. Eleanor Roosevelt to pass through before him, but she refused to go first. She reminded Kennedy, "You are the president!" President Kennedy collected himself and smilingly replied, "I keep forgetting." The former first lady then gently chided him, "But you must never forget."[26] Believers, we must remember who we are and never forget where we stand.

Beeson Divinity School Chapel
13th Annual Pastors School
July 26, 2000

---

26. William Manchester, *Portrait of a President: John F. Kennedy in Profile* (New York: Macfadden-Bartell, 1962), p. 18.

Ascension Sunday Sermon:
This Jesus

Jesus Christ is the same yesterday and today and forever.—Hebrews 13:8

If [people] have pondered the mystery of themselves, they have even more contemplated the mystery of Jesus…yet not all have understood him thoroughly, and their conclusions about him have been diverse."[27] So said one of my seminary professors, Thomas S. Kepler, a saintly believer who had not only a well-stocked mind but a contagious soul. Kepler made the comment more than fifty years ago in introducing his anthology, *Contemporary Thinking about Jesus.* Then, as now—and across the centuries—the public has shown an interest in what reflective thinkers have been saying and writing about Jesus. With a new generation of thinkers now at work, a surge of publications about Jesus of Nazareth has captured even media attention, deepening public interest in this significant subject area.

I am not about to review the continuing debate about the historical Jesus. I stand here as spokesman for a text that speaks signally to our faith and future. This text is all-important for our desired fulfillment. It can help us understand Jesus adequately for confident trust, discipleship, loyalty, and service. I speak about an "adequate understanding" because, in confronting the New Testament truths regarding Jesus, our faith must forever seek understanding since to meet him is to experience mystery. The writer of Hebrews knew this, so he wrote to emphasize the meaning

---

27. Thomas S. Kepler, *Contemporary Thinking About Jesus: An Anthology* (Nashville: Abingdon-Cokesbury Press, 1944), p. 7.

of Jesus for believers: "Jesus Christ is the same yesterday and today and forever." The text holds the summarizing word to a well-written epistle, and it is itself a majestic conclusive for the faith that saves and sustains: "Jesus Christ is the same yesterday and today and forever."

I

In light of all that precedes this passage in the epistle, the writer means that *this Jesus is uniquely distinctive in the plan of God to meet our deepest human need.* This is why he is referred to here as "Jesus *Christ.*" Observe the verbal adjective with care. The title *Christ* is central for understanding *this* Jesus adequately, since he alone was ordained by God as the Anointed One for us.

The personal name *Jesus* was somewhat popular and common among Jews down through the centuries before the Common Era. Scattered references in the works of Josephus list several contemporaries of Jesus who had the same personal name; because this was so, he carefully distinguished between them by way of explanatory comments.[28] One Jesus served as high priest during a part of the Maccabean period, succeeding his dead brother Onias. Strongly influenced by Hellenistic culture, he promoted Greek customs and he even changed his name to Jason, a Greek form. Second Maccabees 4:7 refers to him as ambitious, ungodly, and vile. He was not like *our* Jesus. There was another Jesus, son of See, also a high priest, who served a few years before Annas was appointed. There was a Jesus, son of Damnios, who served as high priest about AD 62–63. Yet another Jesus, son of Gamaliel, served as high priest from AD 63 to 65. Later, a son of Sapphias named Jesus became high priest. All these men bore the name Jesus and gained distinction as privileged priests from vested fami-

---

28. On this see Emil Schurer, *The History of the Jewish People in the Age of Jesus Christ (175 B.C.–A.D. 135)*, new English version revised and edited by Geza Vennes and Fergus Millar, vol. 1 (Edinburgh, Scotland: T. & T. Clark Ltd., 1973), p. 431.

lies. They were noticed, and in some respects notable, in their turn, but not one was like *our* Jesus. Only Jesus of Nazareth bears the title *Christ*.

Jesus was not used as a common name by Jews after the second century, due to their opposition to the church. Christians would not use it because they considered the name too hallowed for any other to wear. A once-common name became rare, being either cursed by unbelievers or viewed as crucial by members of the faith. Jesus Christ holds a uniquely distinctive place in the plan of God. His position shaped human history in the past, continues to influence us in the present, and remains valid for the future: yesterday and today and forever. *This* Jesus holds an unequalled greatness.

However, he is not unchallenged. One German publication fostered by Adolf Hitler's group during his rise to power in Germany stated in audacious sacrilege, "In the centuries to come it will be said by those who look back: 'Christ was great, Adolf Hitler was greater.'"[29] What folly! God used the processes of history to crush both Hitler and his wild claims. General Jodl's remark about Hitler at the Nuremberg trial explains that megalomaniac's greatness. Jodl said, "He was a great man, but an infernal great man."[30] Hitler's life bore the signs of Satan—lying and murder, with a crass disregard for the divine. Hitler himself, a one-time churchman, boasted that his path to "greatness" began when he freed himself from the teachings of the church; he claimed that those teachings fenced him in, saying, "I, too, once had that fence around my soul, but I broke it, stick by stick."[31] What Hitler thought was the way to freedom was really the path to destruction. "There is a way that seems right to a person, but its end is the way to death" says the proverb (14:12).

---

29. Cited from the *Munchener Katholische Kirchenzeitung* (1946), no. 35, p. 27–28.

30. See the discussion by Don Alois Mager, "Satan in Our Day," in *Satan* (New York: Sheed and Ward. 1952), p. 501. Trans. from *Etudes Carmelitaines*, edited by Pere Bruno de Jesus-Maria.

31. As cited in ibid, p. 503.

II

Viewed against the background of this epistle, our text reminds us that *this Jesus is unequivocally divine.* The teachings in this epistle discuss not only the name of Jesus but also his nature.

From the very first sentence in the epistle, the writer of Hebrews was eager to declare this truth about our Lord. He began in earnest, using a rich level of rhetoric; the nature of his facts demanded this. He had an emphasis to make, some essentials to set forth, and some truths to proclaim anew. The divinity of Jesus was one of those truths. Thus this word about our Jesus: "He is the reflection of God's glory and the exact imprint of God's very being, and he sustains all things by his powerful word" (1:3). And this word: "Let all God's angels worship him" (1:6b). And this word: "Your throne, O God, is forever and ever" (1:8a). And this word, "In the beginning, Lord, you founded the earth, and the heavens are the work of your hands" (1:10). And consider this additional word: "Your years will never end" (1:12b). There are still other texts in this epistle that support the writer's declaration about the divinity of Jesus, but enough has been stated to remind us about this truth that has been described as "one of the unborrowed truths of Christianity."[32] Some believers might suggest that this is also Christianity's most unique truth.

III

The text also reminds us that *this Jesus is unavoidably decisive for our personal human destiny.* This fact is stated and restated throughout this epistle, and it forms the very central message of the entire New Testament. From the very first book, the New Testament makes this assertion and presents pertinent facts to support it. The Christologies of the apostles and other

---

32. James Moffatt, *A Critical and Exegetical Commentary on the Epistle to the Hebrews* (Edinburgh, Scotland: T. & T. Clatk. 1952), p. 6.

early Christian writers have one thing common among them: that this Jesus is God's decisive agent in the world. Daniel T. Niles rightly commented that "the Christian faith is more than a Jesus religion. It is concerned with the consequence to [people] of who Jesus is."[33]

The New Testament message deals with the need for people to know that consequence, act on it, and progressively announce it until the rest of the world has heard it and been invited to act upon it. All who read the gospels have access to the history on which the message is based and the reason for Christ's coming among us. No one must break any mysterious code to gain access to the open facts that this Jesus was born into a Jewish family (Luke 2:1–7); his legal father was one Joseph, a carpenter (Matt 13:54–56); that other members of the family included brothers and sisters (Mark 6:3f); that although Jesus was doubtless an adept carpenter himself, his major activities were different after he reached thirty years of age (Luke 3:23); that he traveled up and down Palestine preaching, teaching, and healing, talking about the will and ways of God; that he trained a group of chosen disciples to do the same (Mark 3:14–15); that as he did his work, he became a point of controversy and conflict, accused by the religious leaders of his nation of being a troublemaker and a political menace, which finally led to his death at their hands (Luke 23:13–25).

This is a rather simple sketch of the historical facts, but there is more to Jesus' story than this. The Gospels tell us that God was at work in this Jesus, and in a decisively unique way. The Epistles repeat this claim, and so does the book of Acts, which reports how the disciples Jesus trained continued his ministry, effecting results through the authority of his name. Here is a signal statement about this Jesus from one of Peter's heart-searching sermons preserved in the Acts: "There is salvation in no one else, for there is no other name under heaven given among mortals by which we

---

33. Daniel T. Niles, *Upon the Earth* (Boston: McGraw-Hill Book Co., Inc., 1963), p. 63.

must be saved" (4:12). Paul underscored this by declaring that "God also highly exalted him and gave him the name that is above every name, so that at the name of Jesus every knee should bend, in heaven and on earth and under the earth, and every tongue should confess that Jesus Christ is Lord, to the glory of God the Father" (Phil 2:9–11). The statement about his name now being "above every [other] name" amplifies what is meant in saying that he has been exalted: Jesus now holds a new rank of decisive and universal dominion, and this Jesus, raised from death, holds divine appointment as both official and essential Lord over all.[34]

IV

Our text can speak about Jesus as "the same yesterday and today and forever" because time poses no problem to his being nor his mission. Time cannot rob us of his work on our behalf; it cannot cheat us out of the benefits he came to give. Time confines us, and by a fatal death stroke it will finally cancel out our names from among the living. Everything that comes to life, goes by way of death. Jesus also died, but it is historical fact that he also returned, resurrected from the grave, and he continues to minister "through the power of an indestructible life" (Heb 7:16). Time has not changed the person he is nor the position he holds. "Consequently he is able for all time to save those who approach God through him, since he always lives to make intercession for them" (7:25). Time will take us away, but time will not rob us of the relationship Jesus has made possible for us with God; nor will time cheat us out of knowing him as he is. This Jesus is no figure lost in the past. He does not live by being remembered; he lives because he is. This Jesus helps us apprehend God historically, and those who put their trust in him find that he apprehends our personal

___

34. On this, see Peter T. O'Brien, *The Epistle to the Philippians: A Commentary on the Greek Text* [NIGTC] (Grand Rapids, MI: Wm. B. Eerdmans Publishing Co., 1991), especially pp. 237–42.

histories redemptively. Those whom he claims inevitably have no need to try to recapture him.

Controversies over Jesus will continue, and questions about him will continue to be asked. But beyond the questions and the controversies, this Jesus still stands—uniquely distinctive in the plan of God and in relation to human need, indisputably divine in nature, and unavoidably decisive for our personal human destiny.

The New Testament message about Jesus remains the same because his person and work remain the same. Thus the text: "Jesus Christ is the same yesterday and today and forever." Therefore, we have the warning that follows the text: "Do not be carried away by all kinds of strange teachings" (Heb 13:9a). "Through him, then, let us continually offer a sacrifice of praise to God, that is, the fruit of lips that confess his name" (Heb 13:15).

Rankin Chapel
Howard University
Easter Sunday 1995

An Easter Sermon:
Brought Back from the Dead

Now may the God of peace, who brought back from the dead our Lord Jesus, ...make you complete in everything good so that you may do his will, working in you that which is pleasing in his sight, through Jesus Christ, to whom be the glory for ever and ever. Amen.—Hebrews 13:20–21

I

An awesomeness pervades every burial scene. It is heartrending to watch in grief as what remains physically after the death of a family member or friend is lowered respectfully into a grave or prayerfully deposited in a crypt. There is an instinct for silence as one outwardly looks down and inwardly looks up.

The family and close disciples of Jesus felt that awesomeness when he was crucified and his body was laid to rest in a donated tomb. The execution had happened so quickly. The whole experience was so strange, so unsettling, so unexpected. Jesus was dead and the tomb holding his body had been sealed, but still so much of what he meant to them filled their minds and hearts, so the mourners felt that with his leaving, all had been lost. That was how his family and disciples felt and thought when Jesus died, and that thought and feeling haunted them until, three days later, they saw him alive again. Stunned by his reappearance and surprised by the joy it brought, those disciples hurriedly spread the news that Jesus had appeared to them, that he was alive, that he had been brought back from the dead. The reality of his resurrection and revealed presence changed their thoughts, their feelings, their outlook, their lives, and those disciples felt the courage to live. Blessed by Jesus' return, they made an unyielding commitment of themselves and began to forward his ministry by word and deed. Through Jesus they now knew the God who brought him back from the dead, and now they too were busy doing God's will. Their lives were changed "through"—by means of, because of, in honor of—the resurrected Jesus Christ.

II

Jesus came back from the realm of death. He came back actually and bodily. The first disciples saw and heard him in actual form and in living color after he was raised from death. They did not see a phantom figure conjured by an anxious faith. They did not hear an imaginary voice based on strong memories resounding in their grief-wounded consciousness. Jesus came back bodily from death, not as a mere strong hope but as a living person who could be touched and companioned.

Englishman Rudyard Kipling lost a son in battle during World War I. He remained bitter across a span of years, and due to sadness he lapsed into a prolonged silence. During his bereavement, Kipling learned about some mediums who claimed the ability to contact the dead. For a while he was tempted to consult them, wanting so much to hear the voice or have a vision of his dead son, but he wisely resisted it. Later, Kipling wrote a poem in which he rebuked some of his friends for the way they, in their grief, had marched foolishly like the biblical King Saul down "The Road to Endor."

Paining bereavement and loneliness tempt some to seek the voice or vision of one who has died. The pain of bereavement is not easily managed, and many with hurting hearts are tempted to contact the deceased, only to be beguiled by rappings, spurious voices, or moving objects mediums claim as evidences that a dead loved one is trying to talk back from the grave.

There *is* someone who died and has returned to prove himself alive. That someone is Jesus. He is not here now in bodily form, but he was here after being raised from death, and he was plainly seen and clearly heard. He did not return as a vision, nor as a disembodied voice, but in full form as a real person. God brought him back from the dead. As the apostle Peter declared while preaching some days after having seen the resurrected Jesus, "This Jesus God raised up, and all of us are witnesses" (Acts 2:32).

God specializes in what is original, and raising Jesus from the dead was another original deed of his unlimited power. The Christian faith has always taught this, and true believers have always treasured this truth. We do not worry our minds, trying to explain the miracle. It is enough to say, with the first believers and with the writer of our text, God brought our Lord Jesus, the great shepherd of the sheep, back from the dead.

III

Jesus came back from death because death had no authority to hold him. Hear again the apostle Peter, who explained, "God raised him up, having freed him from death, because it was impossible for him to be held in its power" (Acts 2:24).

Jesus came back from death because he is the one God appointed to be "both Lord and Messiah" (Acts 2:36). The crucified Jesus was not a mere man of his time; he is God's resurrected saving agent for the rest of time. He lived among us once—like us, "lower than the angels"—but he is now exalted, "crowned with glory and honor because of the suffering of death" (Heb 2:9). He is now in the presence of God on our behalf, "able for all time to save those who approach God through him, since he always lives to make intercession for them" (Heb 7:25). Those who saw him after his return from death saw a glimpse of the future. Some of that future was seen in his glorified body and his exalted life. These are fundamental facts that those who saw him reported, and these are fruitful truths for our faith and hope.

IV

It is really about the fruits of faith that our text pointedly speaks. The God who brought Jesus back from the dead can work powerfully within us, equipping and readying us for a meaningful life and service in this world. The text is actually a benediction prayer that those who regard it will experience that power.

The resurrection is fixed in history and eternity. The power that brought about the resurrection is real and effective. The text reminds us that God's power that raised Jesus from death can be just as effective in, for, and through us as we live. The experiential outcomes from his resurrection were to be more than sightings of Jesus, however many; those outcomes were to include an ability, by God's working within us, to live like Jesus, an enabling to do "everything good" that God's will outlines, which pleases God and brings "glory" to Jesus. The resurrection is more than a story for faith; the power that affected it is a resource for every believer's life.

> He lives, to bless me with His love;
> He lives, to plead for me above;
> He lives, my hungry soul to feed;
> He lives, to help in time of need.[35]

---

35. Samuel Medley, "I Know That My Redeemer Lives," *Worship the Lord: Hymnal of the Church of God* (Anderson, IN: Warner Press, Inc., 1989), 213.

For Further Study

Books preceded by an asterisk (*) provide homiletical materials and suggestions.

Commentaries

Attridge, Harold W. *The Epistle to the Hebrews* (Hermeneia series). Philadlephia: Fortress Press, 1989.

Barclay, William. *The Epistle to the Hebrews* (Daily Study Bible). Philadelphia: Westminster Press, 1957.

Bowman, John W. *The Letter to Hebrews; The Letter to James; The First and Second Letters of Peter.* (Layman's Bible Commentary). Richmond, VA: John Knox Press, 1962.

Bruce, Alexander Balmain. *The Epistle to the Hebrews: The First Apology for Christianity, An Exegetical Study.* Edinburgh, Scotland: T. & T. Clark, 1899.

Bruce, Frederick F. *The Epistle to the Hebrews* (New International Commentary on the New Testament series). Rev. ed. Grand Rapids: Wm. B. Eerdmans Publishing Co., 1990.

Buchanan, George Wesley. *To the Hebrews: Translation, Comment, and Conclusions* (Anchor Bible series). 2nd ed. Garden City, NJ: Doubleday & Co., Inc., 1976.

Casey, Juliana. *Hebrews* (New Testament Message series). Wilmington, DE: Michael Glazier, Inc., 1980.

Chadwick, G. A. *The Epistle to the Hebrews: A Devotional Commentary*. London: The Religious Tract Society, 1911.

* Chilstrom, Herbert W. *Hebrews: A New & Better Way*. Philadelphia: Fortress Press, 1984.

Cowles, Henry. *The Epistle to the Hebrews: With Notes, Critical, Explanatory and Practical*. New York: D. Appleton & Co., 1878.

* Craddock, Fred. "The Letter to the Hebrews: Introduction, Commentary, and Reflections," *New Interpreter's Bible*, Vol. XII. Nashville, TN: Abingdon Press, 1998.

Davidson, A. B. *The Epistle to the Hebrews: With Introduction and Notes* (Handbook for Bible Classes series). Edinburgh, Scotland: T. & T. Clark, n.d.

Delitzch, Franz. *Commentary on the Epistle to the Hebrews*. 2 Vols. Edinburgh, Scotland: T. & T. Clark, 1871.

Edwards, Thomas Charles. *The Epistle to the Hebrews*. New York: A. C. Armstrong and Son, 1900.

Ellingworth, Paul. *The Epistle to the Hebrews: A Commentary on the Greek Text* (New International Greek New Testament). Grand Rapids, MI: Wm. B. Eerdmans Publishing Co., 1993.

* Evans, Louis H., Jr. *Hebrews* (The Communicator's Commentary). Waco, TX: Word Books, 1985.

Gooding, David. *An Unshakeable Kingdom: The Letter to the Hebrews for Today*. Grand Rapids, MI: Wm. B. Eerdmans Publishing Co., 1989.

Grant, Frederick C. *The Epistle to the Hebrews: in the King James Version with Introduction and Critical Notes* (Harper's Annotated Bible series). New York: Harper & Brothers, 1956.

Guthrie, Donald. *The Letter to the Hebrews: An Introduction and Commentary* (Tyndale New Testament Commentary series). Grand Rapids, MI: Wm. B. Eerdmans Publishing Co., 1983.

Guthrie, George H. *The Structure of Hebrews: A Text-Linguistic Analysis* (Biblical Studies Library). Grand Rapids, MI: Baker Books, 1994.

Hagner, Donald A. *Hebrews* (Good News Commentary series). San Francisco: Harper & Row, 1983.

Hewitt, Thomas. *The Epistle to the Hebrews: Introduction and Commentary* (Tyndale New Testament Commentaries). Grand Rapids, MI: Wm. B. Eerdmans Publishing Co., 1960.

* Hobbs, Herschel H. *Hebrews: Challenges to Bold Discipleship.* Nashville, TN: Broadman Press, 1971.

Hudson, James T. *The Epistle to the Hebrews: Its Meaning and Message.* Edinburgh, Scotland: T. & T. Clark, 1937.

Hughes, Philip Edgecumbe. *A Commentary on the Epistle to the Hebrews.* Grand Rapids, MI: Wm. B. Eerdmans Publishing Co, 1977.

Jewett, Robert. *Letter to Pilgrims: A Commentary on the Epistle to the Hebrews.* New York: Pilgrim Press, 1981.

Johnson, Luke Timothy. *Hebrews: A Commentary* (New Testament Library). Louisville: Westminster John Knox Press, 2006.

* Johnsson, William G. *Hebrews* (Knox Preaching Guides). Atlanta: John Knox Press, 1980.

Kent, Homer A., Jr. *The Epistle to the Hebrews: A Commentary*. Grand Rapids, MI: Baker Book House, 1972.

Kistemaker, Simon J. *Exposition of the Epistle to the Hebrews* (New Testament Commentary series). Grand Rapids, MI: Baker Book House, 1984.

Koester, Craig R. *Hebrews: A New Translation with Introduction and Commentary* (Anchor Bible). New York: Doubleday, 2001.

Lane, William L. *Hebrews 1–8, 9–13*, 2 vols (Word Biblical Commentary, Nos. 47A/47B). Dallas: Word Books, 1991.

Lenski, R. C. H. *The Interpretation of the Epistle to the Hebrews and the Epistle of James*. Minneapolis: Augsburg Publishing House, 1966.

* Lightfoot, Neil R. *Jesus Christ Today: A Commentary of the Book of Hebrews*. Grand Rapids, MI: Baker Book House, 1976.

* Long, Thomas G. *Hebrews* (Interpretation series). Louisville: Westminster John Knox Press, 1997.

Lowrie, Samuel T. *An Explanation of the Epistle to the Hebrews*. New York: Robert Carter & Brothers, 1884.

Moffatt, James. *A Critical and Exegetical Commentary on the Epistle to the Hebrews* (International Critical Commentary series). Edinburgh, Scotland: T. & T. Clark, 1924.

Montefiore, Hugh. *A Commentary on the Epistle to the Hebrews* (Harper's New Testament Commentaries). New York: Harper & Row, 1964.

Morris, Leon. *Hebrews* (Bible Study Commentary series). Grand Rapids, MI: Zondervan Publishing House, 1983.

Nairne, Alexander. *The Epistle to the Hebrews: with Introduction and Notes.* Cambridge, England: Cambridge University Press, 1957.

Narborough, F. D. V. *The Epistle to the Hebrews: with Introduction and Commentary.* Oxford, England: Clarendon Press, 1930.

Neil, William. *The Epistle to the Hebrews: Introduction and Commentary* (Torch Bible Commentaries). London: SCM Press, Ltd., 1955.

Patterson, Alexander S. *A Commentary, Expository and Practical, on the Epistle to the Hebrews.* Edinburgh, Scotland: T. & T. Clark, 1856.

Peake, Arthur S. *Hebrews* (Century Bible series). Edinburgh, Scotland: T. & T. Clark, 1902.

Pfeiffer, Charles F. *The Epistle to the Hebrews.* Chicago: Moody Press, 1962.

*Pitts, James M., ed. *The Way of Faith: Words of Admonition and Encouragement for the Journey, based on the Letter to the Hebrews.* Wake Forest, NC: Chanticleer Publishing Co., Inc. 1985.

Robinson, Theodore H. *The Epistle to the Hebrews* (Moffatt New Testament Commentary series). New York: Harper & Brothers, 1933.

* Roddy, Clarence S. *The Epistle to the Hebrews* (Proclaiming the New Testament series). Grand Rapids, MI: Baker Book House, 1962.

Sadler, M. F. *The Epistles of St. Paul to Titus, Philemon and the Hebrews: With Notes Critical and Practical.* London: G. Bell and Sons, Ltd., 1910.

Sampson, Francis S. *A Critical Commentary on the Epistle to the Hebrews.* New York: Robert Carter & Brothers, 1856.

Smith, Robert H. *Hebrews* (Augsburg Commentary on the New Testament). Minneapolis: Augsburg Publishing House, 1984.

* Turner, George Allen. *The New and Living Way.* Minneapolis: Bethany Fellowship, 1975.

Turner, Samuel H. *The Epistle to the Hebrews in Greek and English: with an Analysis and Exegetical Commentary.* New York: Stanford and Swords, 1852.

Wenham, Alfred E. *Ruminations on the Epistle of Paul the Apostle to the Hebrews.* Glasgow, Scotland: Hulbert Publishing Co., Ltd., 1924.

Westcott, Brooke Foss. *The Epistle to the Hebrews: The Greek Text with Notes and Essays.* Grand Rapids, MI: Wm. B. Eerdmans Publishiing Co., 1980 reprint.

Wickham, E. C. *The Epistle to the Hebrews: with Introduction and Notes.* London: Methuen & Co, 1910.

Wilson, Geoffrey B. *Hebrews: A Digest of Reformed Comment.* Carlisle, PA: Banner of Truth Trust, 1979.

Wilson, R. Mel. *Hebrews* (New Century Bible Commentary). Grand Rapids, MI: Wm. B. Eerdmans Publishing Co., 1987.

Valentine, Fay. *Hebrews, James, 1 & 2 Peter* (Laymans's Bible Book Commentary). Nashville, TN: Broadman Press, 1981.

Other Helpful Studies

Archer, Gleason L., and G. C. Chirichigno. *Old Testament Quotations in the New Testament: A Complete Survey.* Chicago: Moody Press, 1983.

Barth, Markus. *Conversation with the Bible.* New York: Holt, Rinehart and Winston, 1964.

Bruce, Frederick F. *The New Testament Development of Old Testament Themes.* Grand Rapids, MI: Wm. B. Eerdmans Publishing Co., 1968.

Bruce, Frederick F. *The Canon of Scripture.* Downers Grove, IL: InterVarsity Press, 1988.

Childs, Brevard S. *The New Testament as Canon: An Introduction.* Philadelphia: Fortress Press, 1984.

Dodd, Charles H. *According to the Scriptures: The Sub-Structure of New Testament Theology.* New York: Charles Scribner's Sons, 1953.

Ellis, E. Earle. *Prophecy and Hermeneutic in Early Christianity: New Testament Essays.* Grand Rapids, MI: Wm. B. Eerdmans Publishing Co., 1978.

Ellis, E. Earle. *The Old Testament in Early Christianity: Canon and Interpretation in the Light of Modern Research.* Grand Rapids, MI: Baker Book House, 1992.

Filson, Floyd V. *"Yesterday" A Study of Hebrews in the Light of Chapter 13* (Studies in Biblical Theology, sec. series, No. 4). London: SCM Press, Ltd., 1967.

Goppelt, Leonhard. *TYPOS: The Typological Interpretation of the Old Testament in the New.* Grand Rapids, MI: Wm. B. Eerdmans Publishing Co., 1982.

Hay, David M. *Glory at the Right Hand: Psalm 110 in Early Christianity* (Society of Biblical Literature Monograph series, No. 18). Nashville, TN: Abingdon Press, 1973.

Horton, Fred L., Jr. *The Melchizedek Tradition: A Critical Examination of the Sources to the Fifth Century AD and in the Epistle to the Hebrews* (Society for New Testament Studies Monograph series, 30). Cambridge, England: Cambridge University Press, 1976.

Hughes, Graham. *Hebrews and Hermeneutics: The Epistle to the Hebrews as a New Testament Example of Biblical Interpretation* (Society for New Testament Studies Monograph series, 36). Cambridge, England: Cambridge University Press, 1979.

Johnson, Franklin. *The Quotations of the New Testament from the Old: Considered in the Light of General Literature.* Philadelphia: American Baptist Publication Society, 1895.

Kaiser, Walter C., Jr. *The Uses of the Old Testament in the New.* Chicago: Moody Press, 1985.

Kasemann, Ernst. *The Wandering People of God: An Investigation of the Letter to the Hebrews.* Minneapolis: Augsburg Publishing House, 1984.

Kugel, James L. and Rowan A. Greer. *Early Biblical Interpretation* (Library of Early Christianity) Philadelphia: Westminster Press, 1986.

Lindars, Barnabas. *New Testament Apologetic: The Doctrinal Significance of the Old Testament Quotations.* Philadelphia: Westminster Press, 1962.

Lindars, Barnabas. *The Theology of the Letter to the Hebrews.* Cambridge, England: Cambridge University Press, 1991.

Longenecker, Richard. *Biblical Exegesis in the Apostolic Period.* Grand Rapids, MI: Wm. B. Eerdmans Publishing Co., 1975.

McDonald, James I. H. *Kerygma and Didache* (Society for New Testament Studies Monograph series, No. 30). Cambridge, England: Cambridge University Press, 1976.

Metzger, Bruce M. *The Canon of the New Testament: Its Origin, Development, and Significance.* Oxford, England: Clarendon Press, 1987.

Nairne, Alexander. *The Epistle of Priesthood: Studies in the Epistle to the Hebrews.* Edinburgh, Scotland: T. & T. Clark, 1913.

Peterson, David. *Hebrews and Perfection: An Examination of the Concept of Perfection in the Epistle to the Hebrews* (Society of New Testament Studies Monograph series, No. 47). Cambridge, England: University Press, 1982.

Shires, Henry M. *Finding the Old Testament in the New.* Philadelphia: Westminster Press, 1974.

Souter, Alexander. *The Text and Canon of the New Testament.* London: Duckworth, 1912.

Thiselton, Anthony C. *New Horizons in Hermeneutics.* Grand Rapids, MI: Zondervan Publishing House, 1992.

Thompson, James W. *The Beginnings of Christian Philosophy: The Epistle to the Hebrews* (Catholic Biblical Quarterly Monograph series, No. 13). Washington, DC: Catholic Biblical Association of America, 1982.

Vanhoozer, Kevin J. *Is There a Meaning in This Text?* Grand Rapids, MI: Zondervan Publishing House, 1998.

Vanhoye, Albert. *Structure and Message of the Epistle to the Hebrews.* (Subsidia Biblica series, No. 12). Rome: Editrice Pontificio Istituto Bibico, 1989.

Westcott, Brooke Foss. *A General Survey of the History of the Canon of the New Testament*. London: Macmillan and Co., 1881.

Index of Proper Names

T

Taylor, Gardner C. 126, 127, 136
Taylor, Vincent 83
Tertullian 21, 31
Thyen, Hartwig 106
Timothy, companion of Paul 35, 38, 40
Troeger, Thomas H. 137

U

Urmson, J. O. 98

V

Vander Broek, Lyle D. 107
Vermes, Geza 42, 143

W

Wardlaw, Don M. 138
Watkins, Oscar D. 90

Weinrich, William C. 25
Wesley, John 102, 187
Westcott, Brooke Foss 25, 27, 82
Whitefield, George 152
White, J. L. 107
Wiefel, Wolfgang 41
Wikgren, A. 104
Wilken, Robert L. 91
Williamson, H. G. M. 140
Wills, Lawrence 106
Wilson, John 98
Wittgenstein, Ludwig 136

X

Xenophon 175, 176